Another Side of World War II

A Coast Guard Lieutenant in the South Pacific

Juliana Fern Patten

BURD STREET PRESS
SHIPPENSBURG, PENNSYLVANIA

Unless otherwise noted, the illustrations were supplied by the author.

This Burd Street Press publication
was printed by
Beidel Printing House, Inc.
63 West Burd Street
Shippensburg, PA 17257-0708 USA

The acid-free paper used in this book meets the guidelines for permanence and durability of the Committee on Production Guidelines for Book Longevity of the Council on Library Resources.

For a complete list of available publications
please write
Burd Street Press
Division of White Mane Publishing Company, Inc.
P.O. Box 708
Shippensburg, PA 17257-0708 USA

Library of Congress Cataloging-in-Publication Data

Fern, Jules J., 1913-1991.
   Another side of World War II : Coast Guard lieutenant in the South Pacific / [edited by] Juliana Fern Patten.
      p. cm.
   ISBN 1-57249-377-1
   1. Fern, Jules J., 1913-1991--Correspondence. 2. World War, 1939-1945--Naval operations, American. 3. World War, 1939-1945--Personal narratives, American. 4. World War, 1939-1945--South Pacific Ocean. 5. United States. Coast Guard--Biography. 6. Sailors--United States--Correspondence. I. Patten, Juliana Fern, 1951- II. Title.

D773.F47 2005
940.54'59731'092--dc22
[B]

                                                                                    2005053576

I dedicate this book
of extraordinary letters
to their creator, my father,
whose spirit shall always
remain close to me.
They are a testament to
his companionable humor
and goodness which I had the
good fortune of experiencing
as his daughter and
friend for forty years.

Contents

Maps

Acknowledgments

I would like to thank Margaret Shirley of Portsmouth, New Hampshire, and Marianne Zinn from White Mane Publishing Company for their editorial assistance; my sister, Mary Lee Bretz, for her advice regarding the logistics of the publishing world; and my husband and son for their continual encouragement as I plodded through page upon page of my father's often indecipherable scribble, researching the accuracy and orthography of his recorded details.

"WWII Letters Etc. At Fern's Death: Pitch." These were the words my father had printed in bold letters on the top of the box containing over a hundred letters he had written to his mother. She had saved these letters from his two-year assignment in the South Pacific, and it was only after his death that I discovered them amid trunks of memorabilia in his attic. They were in no order—just merely tossed into a box—but they were each still in their original envelopes with a visible postmark and labeled by his mother with the date received. Included in the envelopes were pertinent photographs, documents, and press releases, all adding to the intrigue of my discovery.

An Ohio native, Jules Fern served in the Ohio National Guard 107th Cavalry from 1936 to 1940. During this time he received his BA in English from Xavier University and his MA from the University of Cincinnati, where, after spending one year as a graduate assistant, he joined the faculty as an English instructor.

In 1942 my father attended the U.S. Coast Guard Academy in New London, Connecticut, serving as a cadet on the *Danmark*, a full-rigged training ship. After graduating in 1943 as a candidate for Reserve Commission, he received orders to report to Port Richmond in Philadelphia and soon thereafter to the Patrol Base at Essington, Pennsylvania. February of 1944 landed him at Naval Training School at Ohio State University, which finally led him to his dream: assignment at sea.

This publication includes all his letters from the time he shipped out from Long Beach, California, as a lieutenant (jg) in May 1944 until his return to Seattle in July 1946. Historically, they reach from the time when American forces in the Pacific were moving west toward converging on the Philippines, through the Japanese surrender, and into the decommissioning of many of the participating naval vessels.

The book is divided into three sections, each comprising the letters Lieutenant Fern wrote to his mother from the three different ships to which he was assigned. His duties and, consequently, his experiences and observations vary according to the life he lives aboard each. Interwoven with his account of a Coast Guard officer's daily routine at sea during war, however, is an often intimate observation of the times and places he experiences.

Lieutenant Fern initially served as a supply, commissary, and recognition officer aboard a Coast Guard-manned LST in the South Pacific, which participated in the invasion of Saipan and the Battle of Leyte. His year aboard the *LST 169* encompassed most of the action of his wartime duty. He was then transferred to a gasoline tanker, on which he spent the next six months in the Philippines. During this time the Japanese surrendered to the United States, and new challenges included facing the problems of occupation, reorganization, and reconstruction. Fern's final assignment was aboard the USS *Racine*, a weather patrol frigate, which shipped out from its homeport of Manicani, "which before the war was nothing but a harmless little coconut island."

These letters are a testament to the fact that my father frequently referred to this period as "the highlight of [his] life."

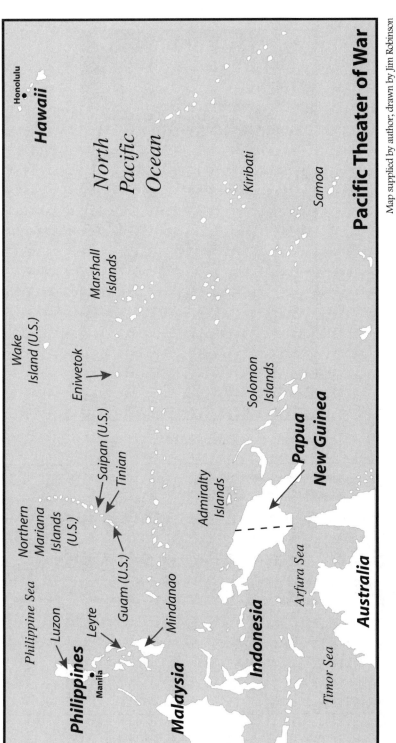

Pacific Theater of War

Map supplied by author; drawn by Jim Robinson

Lieutenant Fern

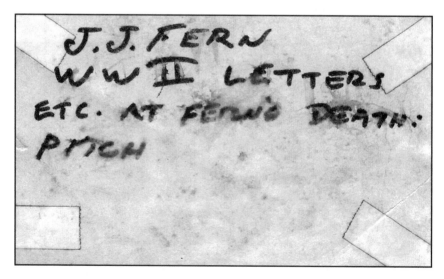

Note taped to top of box containing letters

ARD	Auxiliary repair dock (non self-propelled)
ASW	Anti-submarine warfare
CIC	Combat information center
DUKW	Amphibious truck
LCI	Landing craft, infantry
LCM	Landing craft, mechanized
LCT	Landing craft, tank
LCVP	Landing craft, vehicle and personnel
LSD	Landing ship, dock
LSR	Landing ship, rocket
LST	Landing ship, tank
LVT	Landing vehicle, tracked
PBY	Medium to heavy twin amphibious aircraft
PF	Patrol frigate
PT	Patrol torpedo boat
SP	Shore patrol
VT	Navy torpedo bomber squadron

USS *LST 169*
6 April '44–6 April '45

LSTs (landing ship, tanks) were a naval innovation of World War II due to the need for shallow draft landing craft. They were used to bring transport tanks, jeeps, motorized equipment, food, ammunition, and materiel to our troops in the South Pacific. Delivering large loads to enemy beaches during amphibious assaults, the LSTs allowed troops and vehicles to embark and disembark directly from shore to shore.

Called "Green Dragons" because of their size and color, they were often referred to by their crew as "Large Slow Targets."

The Coast Guard-manned *LST 169*, aboard which Lieutenant Fern served, was launched in February 1943 and commissioned in May 1943. This ship participated in the Gilbert Island Operation of November and December 1943, the capture of Saipan in June and July 1944, and the Leyte invasion in October 1944.

Following the war, the *LST 169* was assigned occupation duty in the Far East until late 1945, decommissioned in 1946, and sold for scrap in 1947. She received three battle stars for service during World War II.

13 May '44

Well—here we are, we 169ers, in the midst of the most incredible collection of aquatic blues, moonlit nights, sparkling days, and lingering sunsets. We left the port from which I called you just a week ago—so you must know that the seabirds have deserted us, and the migrating seals have given us their last quizzical look out of their periscopic faces. Only a few flying fish to remind us of the life beneath the surface of this tremendous expanse.

Convoy courses are, if not circuitous, somewhat out of the ordinary, and we don't see many ships—only our convoy companions and tireless escorts. One gets tired of looking at the sea, wonderful as it is—and begins to survey his ship, his fellow officers, his new duties, the crew, the wardroom, the engine room, the galley, the facilities and the lack of facilities, the recreational facilities and the lack of recreational facilities.

Let's look first at the ship: you've seen pictures of the type, and I can only add that its utilitarian appearance is carried rather consistently to the interior. The staterooms afford the bare comfort of a bunk, a clothes rack, a medicine chest and mirror, and a small book rack. There are no outboard ports, so one relies on blowers and fans for air. The steel bulkheads, steel decks, steel furniture tell one that here is something constructed for an emergency. It is a welder's dream. The wardroom is more of a general utility room than an officer's dining room and lounge. The amenities which one invariably finds in the inner sanctum of the world's crudest service ship are not to be found here. Why, I will tell you later. At any rate I find comfort in my bunk. You recall how I enjoyed reading in bed—and I'm thankful for the learnings.

3

Currently we're rather crowded because we're transporting a batch of new navy men and ten or so officers. In addition, we are transporting an LCT and her crew. This 108ft. craft is secured to our deck. It will be something to get that craft launched from our deck—by induced list. It takes quite a while to get to know your shipmates—which in this case must be officers only, more or less. I'm afraid I might give an unfair appraisal of them at this stage because we are still in the process of learning our new jobs, still a bit too concerned about doing the right thing, and some of us much too concerned about asserting authority to the point of encroaching upon the domains of other people.

My duties are just about what one would expect going aboard a ship with this complement. Six of us had been taking the watch until one was rerouted to new duties—so that leaves five. The man who was to replace him carries some weight, but not in his head, and replaced him for one daytime watch. When it became apparent that he would also have to stand night watches, he calmly announced a change of schedule and eliminated himself from watch standing. I like to stand watches—but four hours often drag, and one gets tired of standing in one place for so long. However, there are many compensations. Last night (I should say this morning), for example, I had the four to eight—which embraced in one watch the beauties of an almost tropical moonlit night, the almost unreal tenderness of a drowsy dawn, and the effulgent beginning of a new day. You see, the bridge is open to the sky. It surmounts all save the mast—and one is put in an excellent position to see each change: each star swing out of position and snuff its light, each morning cloud rouse itself and spread its wings.

I have also been appointed commissary officer and recognition officer. The duties of the former I am familiar with from my tour at Essington. Having good cooks and a seemingly reliable chief commissary steward helps a lot. My recognition duties are just that. At general quarters, practice for which we have every night at sundown, I am supposed to be on the bridge and identifying whatever appears. Since little has appeared, I have not had to extend myself yet.

The wardroom of most ships constitutes a place of private retirement for the officers. This ship was not designed for sociability. Our wardroom is more of a utility compartment in which shop is the main topic at table, in which hangs a bulletin board on which the exec pins an endless stream of signed announcements. I think he was probably a "committee boy" at some West Coast Kiwanis Club or something of the sort. He is always at great pains to start harmless conversations and to laugh at everything obvious, and he would make an excellent candidate for chairman of the Christmas Cheer committee. Our wardroom is painted bold white and looks like a bathroom or laundry. The tables are fast, and sometimes I think it's the White Castle restaurant. The chairs are of stainless steel and imitation leather. But things could be lots worse in that respect—at least it's reasonably clean. Not even linoleum on the deck—just sheet metal.

The engine room is quite impressive: twin screw diesel-powered engines that will turn 800 rpms. But the propellers won't turn that fast. They'll get up to 300—through reduction gears. The engine room is hot, full of valves and gauges and sweating machinist's mates that seem in love with pistons, oil lines and pumps. They are happy below decks—ascend now and then for coffee or a look at the sea, then back to the bowels and the copper colonic system of a power plant.

The galley has one large stove, one large baking machine—diesel-oil heated. Here are made excellent cakes, pies, biscuits, corn bread, white bread. Here whirls the potato peeler that doesn't get the eyes. Here sweat the cooks—two fat ones who nibble all the time; two thin ones who never eat but smoke at every opportunity.

The crew is quartered in a very crowded, unattractive manner. It is too hot below decks where they sleep, and the blowers seem hardly adequate for so large a space. They sleep three deep and try to get sleep amidst banging and blowing and constantly burning lights. On either side of the tank deck—where many trucks and jeeps are comfortably ensconced for the journey—sleep the navy troops.

One popular figure is a dog, which the men picked up as a tiny puppy in Kodiak last year. He is part Labrador—coal black and quite the favorite. At our last port he "jumped ship" for a few minutes, as is his custom, but we changed our berth before he returned. So the men chipped in and offered a $20 reward—his picture was published in the papers—and before we sailed, "Kodiak" was aboard. I really believe that some of the men would not have gone with the ship if he hadn't returned, so highly regarded is he as a symbol of good fortune.

Kodiak

I would like to tell you about the time I visited California and particularly San Francisco. However, I think I've gone on long enough about myself and that I'll tell my impressions of that city at a later date. For the present let me say that I find it in all respects, as far as I could see, a very desirable place. The topography, the cosmopolitan atmosphere, the cleanliness, the air of friendliness that seems to pervade, the flowers, the hill, the Chinese quarter, the churches, the hotels, the stores and shops—the waterfront, Barbary Coast (Saroyan's backgrounds), Telegraph Hill, Nob Hill, the food in the Chinese groceries—roast flattened ducks, rice wine, the Christian atmosphere, the navy atmosphere, ships in the harbor, blue water, Golden Gate, Treasure Island, the endless reaches of poppies, the Oakland bridge, Presidio (the old military fort), the mists rolling in, variety of climate in one city, the restaurants, the taverns, seafood, airplanes, international settlement. Sometime you must see them, ride the cable cars, stroll through Chinatown, have cocktails at Top of the Mark, have seafood at the wharf, drive over the bridges—and get to know a city which is just the right size, seems to harbor nice people, and which is geographically so situated that it has no room for junk and puts it all across the bay in Oakland, much as Cincinnati throws much of its less palatable features to Newport.

Now for you and Cincinnati. You all seem so far away to me—ignorant of the West and the miles involved. Going through Kansas, Oklahoma with its fringe on top, New Mexico, Arizona (Flagstaff), California, was really an experience. Some jaunt. Now I've done it—hit "the Coast." You seem far away, but as one of the quartermasters on watch with me said the other night as we leaned on the bridge rail looking into a star-bathed night: "These stars and the moon certainly hold the world together—my folks see the same moon and the same stars, maybe a few hours earlier, but the same."

It is quite warm in this latitude. Most of the crew goes about in shorts, and I suppose we'll be doing the same soon. My face has peeled once already and is ready for another skinning.

Back to home: I hope the grass hasn't too much of a start and that you've secured the services of a gardener. How is the honeysuckle doing? I suppose the tulips are being riotous, and the lilacs fragrant. (I saw some lovely lilacs in San Francisco. Flower carts and stands on every corner.) Flowers and vegetables in California look like they do on the seed packets. Anyone who sees the carnations and snapdragons and calla lilies and geraniums growing so well so casually out there would give up trying without a hothouse in Ohio.

We must have just changed course and got in the trough—the ship is really rolling. There goes another dish in the officer's pantry. Just so the cold rare roast beef stays intact. I feel sorry for one of the new navy ensigns—he's been pea green for days and has eaten all of one orange since we left.

I am reading *So Little Time* by [John] Marquand and recommend it heartily for you. Does he ever give the present scene a going over! We have a pretty good ship's library, so I won't lack for reading material.

Remember, just a year ago we were in New London and Boston. On May 4 I was commissioned. Time goes by.

Perhaps there'll be some mail at the next stop. I hope so. I hope you get this before July. This is probably a chore to read, but I wanted to give you some idea of things. I'm well and happy, and I love you. Good night.

20 May '44

We've been in this place for a week, and I must say I have had a good look at it. Today I had a rather climactic view of it from the air—an hour and a half's ride in a V4F "Goose"—an amphibious plane which was about to make a test flight just when I arrived to inquire about a sightseeing ride. The pilot cordially invited me to come along—so we buckled our parachutes and were off on one of the most beautiful rides imaginable. All over the famous harbor, out to sea, where the blues and greens and whites take on the most vivid hues. Then swooping down along the coast—over Waikiki, over Doris Duke's fabulous palace by the sea, over the rocky cliffs where the surf flies high and seems to linger, over the heads of spear fishermen and surfboard riders, then inland over volcanic hills and a beautiful valley full of pineapple fields, sugar cane, bananas, breadfruit, and the countless airfields and military posts that dot the island.

The officer's club here is pretty nice. Liquor is scarce, but here one can get it between noon and six. People must be off the streets by ten o'clock, so things cool down rather early hereabouts. In town people line up to get in the bars. Sailors line up to get tatooed. Women are very scarce, and with the exception of natives there are practically none. They manage to have about a dozen American dancing partners at the officer's club. I think they are resident officers' daughters. I had a date with a nice Chinese-Hawaiian the other night. A captain who has lived here for sometime and I went out to the Moana for dinner with our Orientals.

I've never had more laughs than during the last week—with Lieutenant Wira and Ensign Werring. We really took over the town. All we needed was a couple of ukeleles and parrots on our shoulders. At the Royal Hawaiian we simply walked into a room on the second floor that looked like a club room. No one was there, so we opened the icebox and drank all the beer in it. When the steward arrived, we began scrambling around for an excuse, but before we had formulated one, he asked us if we wanted more. At the officer's club you pay for things with coupons. One of the bartenders, who is a seaman's o.c. thinks he knows me from Illinois, so I let him think it. As a result, I have spent exactly 75 cents at the club in one week!

Pineapple fields

24 May '44

We are loaded to the gills, or I guess I should say the gunwales—and above. Lots of nice army officers are aboard and we're having a better time socially, so I don't mind the crowding. The captain likes to play bridge, but I can't help much in that. If only he'd stop being so worrisome, he'd be good company. When you get him off the subject of the ship, he's very interesting. I think he is too afraid of the bigwigs in the navy. That is a mistake. They ride you all the more if you let them think you're afraid of them.

I must hit the sack now. I've got a lot of pineapples to stow tomorrow. Are they delicious! Give my best to all.

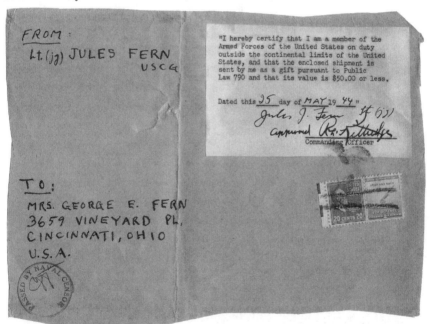

Wrapping from package, probably containing "Japanese souvenirs," sent by Jules Fern to his mother, Mrs. George E. Fern

7 June '44

It has been some time since I wrote you and some time since I've heard from you, but since we arrived here this morning, we are all anxious to see if the floating post office has anything for us, and of course I want to write you and tell you a bit of what we have been doing, without violating censorship regulations.

This morning I had the four-to-eight watch and had the thrill of seeing another priceless southwest Pacific night undergo the miraculous transformation into a dawn of a thousand colors. The full moon—and the magnificence of the rising sun—then landfall, after thirteen days at sea, continuous running in a large convoy, zigzagging, maneuvering, turning, signal drill, firing, abandon ship drill, collision drill, firing small arms at boxes, cans, etc. So this morning there loomed up a little group of islands, an atoll, whose name I wish I could tell you so you could follow it on the map. But you'll have to guess where for the time being. An atoll is a reef found by the rim of a sunken volcano crater. Little animals which extract lime from the water build their myriads of little houses out of the lime they extract. This makes coral, and eventually the rotting coral plus the subsoil, which is rotted lava, produce soil and sand and palm trees and beaches. This particular place was stormed by the Americans last fall and now serves as an advance base. When we take on more provisions, we will steam on another 1,300 miles and hope to accomplish something. (There goes the dinner bell—slight pause.)

These islands are small, none of them more than a mile long—full of palm trees and little else, I suppose. They remind me of the kind of island one reads about and hopes to settle upon one day in order to get away from it all. One of the group has been shelled so badly that there are no leaves on the palm trees—just bare sticks.

The trip out here has been very pleasant. We are carrying an artillery battalion, including twenty-three officers. They are really a rather exceptional group. Almost all of them are National Guard officers from a New York City regiment. The fact that I was in the NG creates a bond right there, so I get along with them excellently. We talk a lot about its merits—and we are all more or less agreed that the best officers and men in the army are those who were in the National Guard before. Why? Because anyone who is interested enough in the defense and integrity of the country in peacetime will certainly be more conscious of it in wartime and in a more effective way. When you figure it out, we in the 107th Cavalry had more soldiering, maneuvering, training, etc. in our weekly periods, weekend trips, summer camps and occasional large maneuvers, than the so-called regular soldier had in a like period. For years the regular army sat comfortably on and at various posts, working as little as possible. Most NG men are of the calibre that feel it's a part of a gentleman to be ready for military service. Milton in his "Essay on Education" included military life to some degree as a necessary part of the whole man.

One of these men whom I like very much is a Fordham graduate. He is very droll, never worries, doesn't give a hoot what people think—but then doesn't have to because he's usually right. We've been having nightly beer and anchovies in my stateroom. Some of them brought rum and whiskey, so I get the steward to whip us some Planter's Punches now and then. Last night the steward made a beautiful tray of sandwiches. Isidio Idencio, the Philippino, prepares my meat especially rare and cooks Japanese omelets with dried shrimp—and always has something for me. Bacigalupi treats me well too. He wakes me gently, then brings coffee to me in bed.

One of the amusing things on a ship is the means the men resort to to get an alcoholic drink. They save the juice from canned fruits, put sugar and yeast in it, and in four days have a really potent concoction. The engineers invariably rig up a distilling apparatus and use anything, including fermented grape jam, watered, to produce the alcohol. I brought several pineapples aboard in our last port and put them on the shelf in my room. After a week one of them exploded and showered the room with a very strong juice. So the steward took it and showed me how you can cut out the core, put in a little sugar and yeast and have a good drink.

(It is now 2 AM 8 June.)

Just returned from eight hours of chasing around the harbor with a provision boat. I arrived at the provision ship and was asked to dinner. Large wardroom, comfortable appointments, chicken dinner, fresh strawberry shortcake. Provision-ship people live well. They carry all kinds of food, frozen fruits, vegetables—all the best. We are taking so much food aboard we hardly have a place to stow it. But I guess we'll need it. We now have enough for 120 days.

I hear by the radio that France has been invaded. Also that Rome was invaded.

If I had an easy time at Essington, I'm making up for it now. I am senior watch officer—stand four hours on the bridge out of every 20;

commissary officer—plan the meals and purchasing; recognition officer—we have daily classes now, with some equipment I got in the last port. I also am auditing officer for the officer's mess and the ship's service store—and lately have been assisting the captain with reading the endless stream of directives, plans, logistics tables, etc.

If I get a chance tomorrow, I'm going swimming off the bow. The water is so blue and riveting. But I must stay up all night to see that our provisions get aboard. The men have a habit of hiding when they get tired—even on the brink of an important moment.

It is warm in Cincinnati, I suppose. I hope it's not as hot as it is here. I go about in shorts much of the time. All of us drip and look like stokers, but we'll get used to it.

If you don't hear from me for awhile, don't worry. There may not be any place to send mail. Good night.

9 June '44

Yesterday I had the pleasure of receiving three letters from you and a variety of interesting clippings. The mail service is really good to these outlying bases. The big Coronados come twice a day, bearing tons of mail for the thousands of men afloat and ashore. We took our small boat ashore to the post office for the fleet and walked around an encampment that is almost a city—yet three months ago it was the battleground that resulted in our obtaining a strategic airstrip. The coconut trees are bare sticks, but the Seabees use them for telephone poles, and set up transportation facilities and communications, put up tents, huts, barns for canteens and supplies—beer, candy, officer's club—it's really wonderful the way they accomplish things and get them in running order. In spite of all the waste and inefficiency, when there is a job to be done, it seems to get done. On this mile-long atoll island, at no point more than 300 yards wide, are now quartered many troops. Here too is a chapel—little, prefabricated Gothic affair.

We are shoving off today for other shores. Do you remember my speaking of a girl in Cincinnati named Marianna Cox? I always think of her in connection with our destination.

I must go now. Love to all.

Northern Mariana Islands

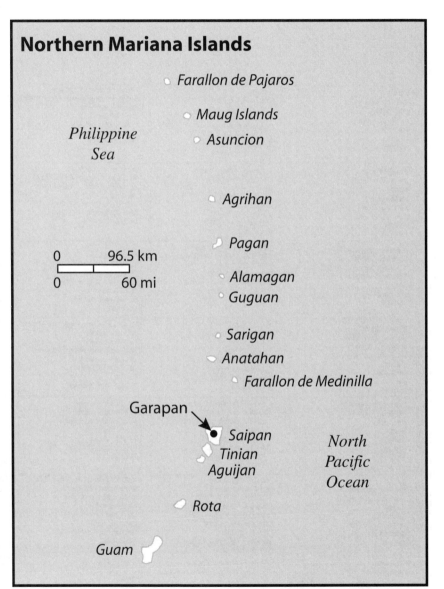

Farallon de Pajaros

Maug Islands

Philippine Sea

Asuncion

Agrihan

Pagan

0 ———— 96.5 km

0 ———— 60 mi

Alamagan

Guguan

Sarigan

Anatahan

Farallon de Medinilla

Garapan

Saipan

Tinian

Aguijan

North Pacific Ocean

Rota

Guam

Map supplied by author; drawn by Jim Robinson

S. and A. Form No. 333
October 1939

BILL OF FARE FOR THE GENERAL MESS

U.S.S. ...LST 169...(50169)....................

Week beginning ......19 June.. .. .., 1944

	BREAKFAST	DINNER	SUPPER
MONDAY			
TUESDAY	Fruit Cereal and milk Hot cakes Pork sausage Butter Syrup Coffee	Steak Grilled onions Rissole potatoes String beans Sliced tomatoes Fruit salad Bread and butter Iced chocolate	Steamed frankfurters Boiled lima beans (Ham hock) Fried potatoes Cole slaw Chocolate cake Bread and butter Orangeade
WEDNESDAY	Fresh fruit Cereal and milk Bacon Fried eggs Hot rolls Jam Butter Coffee	Breaded pork chops Boiled potatoes Cream sauce Creamed corn Applesauce Fruit jello Bread and butter Iced tea	Soup and crackers Beef stew (egg dumplings) Spinach (egg garnish) Vegetable salad Chocolate ice cream Bread, butter, & jam Lemonade
THURSDAY	Canned grapefruit Cream of wheat Creamed chipped beef Toast (Buttered) Jam Chocolate Coffee	Fresh fried shrimp French baked potatoes Creamed peas Vegetable salad Strawberry ice cream Rolls and butter Tea	Soup Veal cutlets Mashed potatoes Country gravy Buttered asparagus Cold tomatoes Bread and butter Peaches Coffee
FRIDAY	Fresh fruit Cereal and milk Poached eggs Hash (Catsup) Toast Butter Jam Coffee	Roast beef Boiled potatoes Brown gravy Kernel corn Sliced tomatoes Blackberry pie Bread and butter Orangeade	Vegetable soup and crackers Salmon salad Potato salad Boiled lima beans (Bacon) Sliced tomatoes Stuffed olives Fruit Bread and butter
SATURDAY	Fresh grapefruit Oatmeal and milk Hot cakes Bacon Butter Syrup Coffee	Virginia baked ham Raisin dressing Mashed sweet potatoes Green peas Vegetable salad Ice cream Rolls and butter Iced tea	Salisbury steaks Barbecue sauce French fried potatoes Snap beans Fruit salad Bread and butter Coffee
SUNDAY	Fruit Cereal and milk Soft boiled eggs Bacon Biscuits Butter and jam Tomato juice Coffee	Roast chicken Mashed potatoes Giblet gravy Creamed peas and carrots Celery and Ripe olives Cranberry sauce Fruit jello Rolls, butter, & jam Iced chocolate	Chicken soup and crackers Boston baked beans Cold cuts and cheese Potato salad Chilled tomatoes Canned fruit Rolls, butter, & jam Iced tea

Total estimated cost .... Total estimated rations .... Estimated ration cost per day ....

APPROVED:

R. L. KITTREDGE
Lieutenant USCGR
........................, U.S.N.,
Commanding.

Respectfully submitted,

J. J. FERN
Lieutenant (j.g.) USCGR
.... Supply Corps, U.S.N.,
Supply Officer.

16—11590

Menu prepared by Lieutenant Fern
in his duty as commissary officer

21 June '44

The first day of summer—the summer solstice—and I am thinking of how hot it probably is in Cincinnati, but breezy of course. Knee deep in June.

It is rather hot here too—and I suppose it always is. I think I can safely tell you where we are now. We are beached on a reef at Saipan—a beautiful island in the Marianas. The reef is a thousand yards off shore, and we are situated ideally to watch a real war. We came from Eniwetok—where we took on more provisions—to this island under heavy screen of battleships and cruisers and all kinds of fighting ships. About three days ago we arrived—then withdrew, then arrived, then withdrew—and now we are here, discharging our own cargo of big guns, ammunition, DUKWs, LVTs, LCVPs, jeeps, tractors—and men. During the withdrawing periods we were bombed twice by the Japanese, but the bombs never landed closer than 700 yards. The anti-aircraft fire that our convoy put up made any pyrotechnic display that I've seen look ridiculously small.

Now the great jaws of dozens of LSTs are open—and the soldiers are pouring forth. The Greeks and their thousand ships—the Trojan horses, the camouflaged ships that look like islands—suddenly opening their great maws to emit the clamor of war and the clanging of Apollo's arrows. I forget the wonderful onomatopoeic line in the *Iliad* describing Apollo and his arrows. I have it marked in one of my books. I can't help thinking of the Greeks every time I look about me. The whole thing seems so simple and elementary. There is practically no air power operative now, and all the operation is performed fundamentally, just as the invasion of Britain by the Normans and of Ireland by the Phoenicians and of Troy by the Greeks and of Cuba by the Spaniards and of the Philippines by the Americans and of Carthage by the Romans. The infantry goes in small boats and tractor-type vehicles (which are better because of the reefs), tanks follow, a beachhead is established, then mortar platoons, then the artillery. Only thing lacking is the cavalry, which I think would do well here because of the hills and snipers.

This beachhead was established at no small cost. The Japanese tactic is to allow invasion, then snipe and draw in. Last night they succeeded in blowing up our largest ammunition dump. They sit in the mountains of Tapotchau and can see the whole island —25 x 3 miles—and press buttons that set off prearranged charges. They don't reveal their positions very often. The beachhead is now more than that. We have the southern, less hilly end of the island. Yesterday I went ashore three times, and once got to the front lines and saw some real fighting. It's my first experience with war—but I can't get over how calmly a fact imposes itself upon one. I found myself searching houses that hadn't been touched—walking with a drawn pistol into stables and outhouses—looking nonchalantly at piles of dead Japanese, standing blandly in the midst of the roar of artillery and machine gun fire, watching the medics bring in their pitiful cases, then the lines of prisoners, and the burials, and the stockades full of sobbing women and bewildered children. I brought back quite a few souvenirs which I may get to send home someday. Among them a Garand rifle, which I am glad to have, as much as I regret the occasion which permits me to have it.

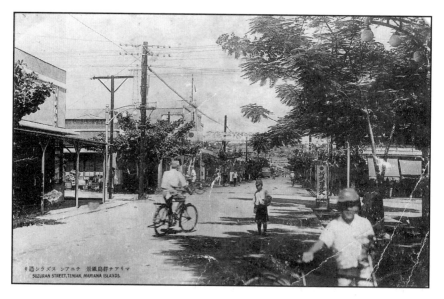

Suzuran Street, Tinian, Mariana Islands

23 June '44

And what a dream is this night. The unbelievable beauty of an almost tropical night, mixed with the vastly exciting display of belligerent

BELIEVE IT OR NOT   By Ripley

(Reg. U. S. Pat. Off.)

DEWEY BRICKER
TRUE NAME OF
A RAILROAD CONDUCTOR
IN Frankfort, Ind.

**WALNUT WITH
3 DISTINCT SECTIONS**
Found by
CHESTER ANDREWS
Bethlehem, Pa.

**QUEEN
MARIANA**
OF SPAIN
AFTER WHOM THE
MARIANA ISLANDS
IN THE PACIFIC WERE NAMED

WAS THE FIRST QUEEN TO USE COSMETICS!
WHEN SHE LEARNED THAT THE NATIVE WOMEN WORE NO CLOTHES - IT
CAUSED HER TO BLUSH SO SHE APPLIED POWDER TO HIDE BLUSHES THEREAFTER
SHE WAS ALSO THE FIRST SPANISH QUEEN TO WALK IN PUBLIC AND FIRST TO LAUGH IN PUBLIC

Daily Pacifican, 11 October 1945

force. We have been in this area for seven days and nights, and now we are anchored half a mile from the Japanese lines on the beautiful island ahead of us. Here we are in a box seat for the greatest show I've ever seen. The shells are whizzing, star shells are lending a carnival glare to the mountain tops. To our left a great naval battle is taking place—the big guns of the fleet booming out and illuminating the sky. Why do we stay here? Because daily we must put ashore additional cargo and ammunition from the larger deep-draft vessels that lay behind the harbor area. All our army has disembarked, and I keep watching their progress through the day from the deck through the glasses we have. It all seems so remarkably plain—one can see a company of infantry surround a clump of trees, then move in with mortar fire and rifle fire, then the big howitzers behind lob shells into enemy positions. The island is full of subterranean passages. Caves all over the hills. Methodically, the artillery covers the area—foot by foot, leaving a network of shell holes. Less than a mile from us is a little town that is still held by the Japanese. The shells pour into it, houses are ablaze—but the natives hold out. Seasoned Japanese infantry men from Tokyo have been sent in. Ten years' experience as a fighting unit!

I have visited our artillery position five times—always at dusk—because it seems that is the only time I could get away. I usually have to sneak off because Captain Kittredge is so extremely cautious and won't let us go ashore anymore. The other night I went ashore to take some coffee and fruit to some officers whom I befriended on the ship. While I was at their shelter—foxholes with palm leaves over them—a sentry came running over to say that snipers were 500 feet away. We all dropped to the ground, the "ducks" that were unloading our ship were stopped, and it looked like I was there for the night. Then another sentry came and reported more snipers. Then the crack of rifles, carbines—then deadly silence. For three hours we lay there—I had only a .45 pistol with me—until the "ducks" began to run again. Then I caught one back to the ship. It was pretty exciting, but I enjoyed it and really wished I was in the army. I often think I should have stayed with my first love. It gives you the feeling that you're really in the part that counts primarily. I constantly think how really elementary the war of aggression is—in spite of air power and all the mechanical advances. No amount of bombing actually takes a country or even a little twelve-mile island. When I think of the soldiers going through the war every day and every night, living on warm water and the simplest K rations—of no baths or showers, of dust a foot thick, of sleeping in a measly foxhole and enduring the relentless attack of flies and mosquitoes—I feel it is hardly fair for me to live in such comparative luxury. Of course there is a lot we have to do, and if they get the range on us from the shore or the air, there isn't much we can do about it. And then the watches at night are no picnic—the ever-present danger of fire, explosion, and collision. It's quite a responsibility to take the deck, and I sometimes think how very nice it is for all the people below to rely on me during my watches.

But somehow all these things seem so terrible when you read about them—and so matter of fact when they come upon you. I can't feel the glimmer of alarm. Maybe it's my nature, low blood pressure and all, but I'm inclined to think that it's more a matter of thinking a thing through and using reason in the approach—plus, of course, faith in God and, above all, an attitude of compliance with His will.

One of the battery positions found two large wooden kegs buried in the ground. They told me about it, so I went ashore to get them. We thought it was sake. As a matter of fact, I was hiding behind them during the sniping. When we got them back to the ship, the pharmacist's mate who went with me hid them in the bilges. Then we descended like thieves to open them and have an orgy. What luck. Nearly lost our lives over two kegs of soy sauce, which the Japs use on rice. It is delicious sauce, better than you buy in the States. Our Philippino steward pays 45 cents a pint for it. There are about twenty gallons in this loot. I think I'll bottle it and sell it to him. The pharmacist's mate and I were going to sell it for $5 a shot if it were sake—what with what we went through to get it. All I could think of as I lay behind the kegs was someone saying, "That stuff will be the death of you yet." Mayo, the pharmacist's mate, and I were laughing so hard we began to constitute a menace to safety. If Captain Kittredge knew we were ashore and, on top of it, what happened, he'd have us both drawn and quartered. He won't even let the officers drink the beer they brought aboard. That's where I fooled him. I shared mine with the National Guardsmen and enjoyed it. I have only five bottles left. I have four bottles of sake, which is convenient. I traded fresh fruit with some marines for it. Being commissary officer has its advantages. Today we had the rarest, tenderest roast beef. That is, mine was rare—because Idencio knows I like it that way.

It seems so unreal, sitting here talking to you, listening to these big guns that never stop. So far away, yet so near.

It's about ten o'clock this midsummer's night, and before I go on deck, I must inspect the galley. Tomorrow, Saturday, the captain will go through, looking under the icebox for roaches and rubbing his hands on the forks for grease. War or no war, the inspections must go on. He really inspects, I'll say that for him. He gets into the most ridiculous positions looking for dirt, but usually manages to find it. He practically crawls in the oven. Typical ruse in the storeroom to keep him out is to disinfect with formaldehyde. Burns the eyes so you can't see or even stay in the place.

I must close now. This will go to the mail ship tomorrow and I hope be in your hands before the 4th of July. Happy Independence Day to all. Don't worry now. I'm just leading a full life and loving every minute of it.

USS *LST 169*

Saipan, June 1944
Troops disembarking from USS *LST 169*

Saipan, June 1944
Launching of the *LCT 1061* from deck of *LST 169*

Saipan, June 1944
Dust on the beach is from artillery fire

Saipan, June 1944
Taken from *LST 169*

2 July '44

Tonight we are anchored about a mile off shore, and a beautiful moon is bathing a scene of what must be terror for many of those lying in foxholes all over the southern half of Saipan. Nights are the worst, according to the dozens of soldiers I've talked with since we've been here. It's then that the Japanese come out in their rubber-soled (separate big toe) shoes and creep through the lines. There are still plenty of Japanese on the island, and I suppose the last few days will be filled with blood for the 22,000 that still remain—hidden in massive caves in the hills, in the woods, in the town of Garapan.

I can hardly believe that I am able to participate in such an adventure as this—so much sooner than I had anticipated—and to such all-around advantage for me. Advantages include the facts that this is the toughest action so far in the Pacific as far as men in battle are concerned, that I have had a box seat anywhere from a quarter of a mile to five miles off shore for the whole thing from the very beginning, that the island may be easily comprehended—and the movement of the armies over the terrain can be followed with the long glass or binoculars. I spend about four hours every day just watching the actions, and I must say that no one could hope to see a better show. It sounds a little like Nero, doesn't it? But it's not as simple as that, because every night we have bombing raids during which we're all more or less expecting to be hit. Anti-aircraft fire is not too efficient, and it's only rarely that we see planes shot down. But it's nothing like lying in a foxhole a few hundred feet from the enemy.

Additional advantages include the fact that I have managed by some way to get ashore several times, and live for a time the life of a soldier. It makes me wish very often that I had stayed in the cavalry, but then when I think that I can come back to the ship, get a shower and a good meal and a clean bunk, I guess I'm better off. But the plain fact is that there can be nothing more thrilling than front-line action—taking shots at the enemy and matching your individual skill against his.

And this war, this Saipan war, seems to be largely individual—and almost old-fashioned. There is very little aircraft involved as yet; during the first few days there was practically none. It is mostly a matter of establishing a foothold—and that was done with plenty of lives, I can assure you—and then digging in with nothing more than rifles and machine guns, a few mortars, a few light tanks for support, and hoping the artillery behind will get the range. But here the artillery didn't get ashore for three days, and this country is too mountainous for mobile tanks. It is all a very simple thing— and our forces can be thankful that the Japanese have blossomed out with no super weapons or that they have not appeared with any superior artillery equipment. I would love to see a regiment of horse cavalry working with and in advance of the infantry. This is perfect country for it, and, I believe, the terrain which demands it. But military authorities have been caught in the net that excludes anything non-mechanical—as far as mobility is concerned. Yet they are certainly forced to admit that here men's legs are counting more than any motorized equipment. I have watched the battle for Sunday Hill as I call it—not a big hill, but bare and pockmarked from shelling—for seven days, from last Sunday to this Sunday. It is a constant advance and retirement, where cavalry, fast-moving, would certainly be more at an advantage than men who must rely on their own feet—this in hot climate with heavy fighting equipment.

Last Thursday I spent most of the day on the front, and finally succeeded in seeing Japanese soldiers darting about—in the outskirts of Garapan—a town of about 10,000. Here it is hand to hand, house to house. I went ashore where I was turned over to a Lieutenant Spaulding, a public relations officer, who took me in a jeep to another major who gave me permission to look up a sergeant. When I found him—about five hundred yards from the front—he was calmly repairing a Japanese bicycle. He introduced me to his lieutenant, and he agreed to my joining them as they were going to the front for six hours. Before we went, he showed me a box of beautiful Japanese officers' swords, which his men had taken from captured and fallen Japanese officers. The men who take them tag them, and then they are sent to their homes if they themselves are killed. He also showed me some of their loot—sake, beer, brandy— and later on presented me with a good supply. We rode up in his jeep and gradually relieved the men at the front. They were behind sandbags, in houses, scattered in various positions that were more or less a horizontal E and W line, and I stayed with the sergeant in a house. I had my Garand rifle and a .45 pistol—but all that day did not have a chance to use them. It was quiet, but twice we saw Japanese soldiers darting from one house to another, as the shells that were dropping from behind us caused them to scatter. The big shells of the 105 howitzers were being sent just two hundred yards ahead of us, scattering shrapnel in every direction. These, I knew, were being fired by the artillery battalion we brought over from Oahu. We were quite comfortable in the coral-block four-room house. We sat on grass mats and watched through every available opening. Chickens and goats strolled about, oblivious to everything. The well-organized ordnance were combing the area for all arms, Japanese and American, and the MPs were gathering the sake into trucks. So since this has been the way things are—there isn't too much in the way of souvenirs. A week earlier, all one had to do was walk around and pick up rifles, carbines—souvenirs of any kind. But souvenir hunters get hurt and in the way, and the soldiers drink too much sake if they don't take it away.

It seemed so normal—not normal, but matter-of-fact rather—to be there. Occasionally a Jap mortar shell would land near us and throw rubble against the house, but other than that nothing happened, and at five o'clock we were relieved, and the men went back to their bivouac, which was not more than a thousand yards down the beach road. I think one of the things that makes everything seem so calm is the eternal sunshine. The weather is so positive, and there is little of that What Price Glory business of mud and rain. Instead, it's impenetrable dust—clouds—on the ground 18 inches deep, soft and gritty dust that covers everything and gets caked on your face from the mixture with sweat. Back at the bivouac we all bathed in the ocean and then caught an LVT (tank) back to the ship.

My only souvenirs, but much prized, are a Japanese company guidon we found in a Japanese tank that had been knocked out, and a pair of chopsticks I took out of a Japanese soldier's pocket. Incidentally, the burying program is much better than it was. The Japanese are burying a lot of their own dead, and our forces do the rest, using Japanese prisoners. Our own dead are quickly removed. There have been lots of casualties, and the chaplains and graves-registration outfits are kept busy. At first the dead soldiers were buried where they fell, with the result that many of the bivouac areas and foxholes are located side by side with the white crosses. Each of the aggressor divisions has its cemetery behind the lines. We can see the one for the 2nd Marine Division, which has the west side of the island—rows and rows of white crosses. The Japanese are simply dumped in shell holes and covered over.

All these things seem so terrible when you read about them in the papers. There is something about print and broadcasts that makes facts more frightening than they are. Being in the midst of them, one has no room for emotional reactions, and that's the only way I can explain how one can calmly look at a truckload of soldiers with mangled legs and hands, at graves side by side with foxholes—at the utter desolation of a bombed and shattered remnant of what was once a peaceful city.

Two days ago I went over to a transport for supplies, and visited the sick bay too. Here were three hundred wounded men, lying in their bunks waiting to go back to Oahu. Somehow when they get bandaged it doesn't seem so bad. One of the lieutenants we brought over here, Blumer (he and I worked together because he was mess officer for the army troops), had the misfortune early in the campaign to lose a leg. I haven't visited their positions lately, so I don't know how the others are faring, but I hope to get a chance to go over tomorrow.

We are lying to in the harbor, taking on damaged tanks and empty shell cases. I suppose when we get a load, we'll go back to Pearl Harbor and prepare for another invasion.

Today is Sunday, so we made arrangements for a church liberty party. We took a boat over to the transport *Cambria*, which is Coast Guard manned. We all went to confession, Mass and Communion, then came back, had a turkey dinner and spent the afternoon swimming and visiting with the officers of a destroyer that came alongside to give us her empty shell cases.

Tonight the big guns are blasting away. Each concussion shakes the ship, and we are speculating on how much longer it will take to secure the island. And then what? There are other islands in this group. All I can say is that this is certainly an adventure and experience, plus the opportunity to see things that I wouldn't want to miss.

I have the four-to-eight watch tomorrow, and we are beaching near the lines at Garapan to take on some more damaged LVTs at 5:30—so I better get some sleep. Besides, we'll probably have to get up in the middle of the night for general quarters if the planes come over, which they probably will. The other night when a plane was shot down after much firing, a cheer went up over the island and harbor that would beat any Ohio State Football Bowl cheer. Spontaneous too.

I got some nice chutney from the supply ship the other day. Tomorrow we are having roast beef, so I shall break it out. I eat too much out here. I think I'll go on a diet.

If I go ashore tomorrow, I'll take some fresh fruit. It goes a long way in getting by the MPs [military police]. The favorite MP punishment for souvenir hunters is to put them in a burial gang for Japanese soldiers who have been dead for days. It's not very pleasant, but the stench that came off that island for the first week was worse than Mill Creek could ever have been. In Garapan it's still that way and will be until the battle is over.

Tell Buddy I have a Japanese map for Caroline, which I got out of a schoolhouse. Also some pottery for Mrs. E. Hope I can get it home. Give my best to Ruth. I have a Japanese soldier's jacket, which Stephen might like to have. The other night I ate rice with chopsticks in a rice bowl while dressed in a kimono and burning incense. Also had some sake. All one day's loot. Good night.

12 July '44

At Eniwetok a few days ago, we received our mail, and I received a gratifying pile of letters, mostly from you, and needless to say, was delighted by each of them. I had letters from early in June, and one from Louis dated as late as July 3.

We have been having more opportunities to get to Mass and Communion. Last Sunday we were anchored at Eniwetok and blinked around until we found a ship with a Catholic chaplain, then requested permission to send a church party over. We found a ship less than two hundred yards away, the USS *Ajax*, which is a repair ship with a complement of 1,500 men. Some ship. It carries a complete machine shop. The interior looks like a large machine-tool plant. We had Mass, general absolution, and Communion on the top deck under a canvas awning. It was very breezy, and the priest gave a good sermon. The week before we had Mass on the USS *Cambria*, a transport, at Saipan anchorage.

We left Saipan the following day, and the battle was still raging. I hear now that the island is conquered, except for snipers—who sometimes stay around for months, hiding in underground passages. I rather hated to leave without seeing the men we brought over again. Maybe

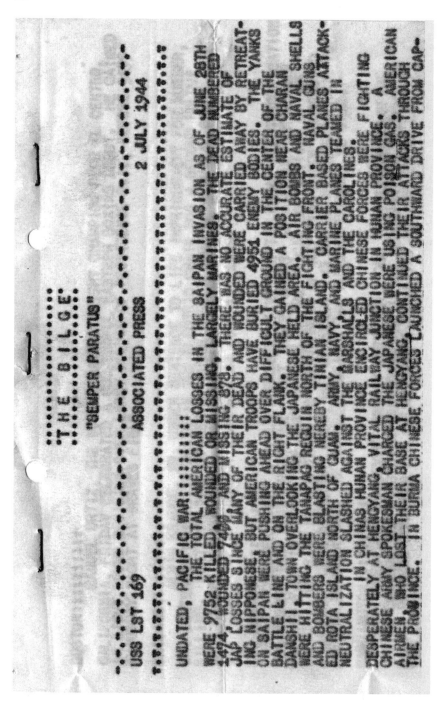

T H E B.I.L.G.E.
"SEMPER PARATUS"

USS LST 169

ASSOCIATED PRESS

2 JULY 1944

UNDATED, PACIFIC WAR:::::::::
THE TOTAL AMERICAN LOSSES IN THE SAIPAN INVASION AS OF JUNE 28TH WERE 9752 KILLED, WOUNDED OR MISSING. LARGELY MARINES. THE DEAD NUMBERED 1474, WOUNDED 7400, AND MISSING 878. THERE WAS NO ACCURATE ESTIMATE OF JAP LOSSES SINCE MANY OF THEIR DEAD AND WOUNDED WERE CARRIED AWAY BY RETREATING NIPPONESE. BUT AMERICAN TROOPS HAVE BURIED 4951 ENEMY BODIES. THE YANKS ON SAIPAN WERE PUSHING AHEAD OVER DIFFICULT GROUND IN THE CENTER OF THE BATTLE LINE AND ON THE RIGHT FLANK. THEY GAINED A POSITION NEAR CHARAN DANSHII TOWN OVERLOOKING THE JAPANESE HELD AREA. AIR BOMBS AND NAVAL SHELLS WERE HITTING THE TANAPAG REQUIR NORTH OF THE FIGHTING FRONT. NAVAL GUNS AND BOMBERS WERE BLASTING NEREBY TINIAN ISLAND. CARRIER BASED PLANES ATTACKED ROTA ISLAND NORTH OF GUAM. ARMY, NAVY AND MARINE PLANES TEAMED IN NEUTRALIZATION SLASHED AGAINST THE MARSHALLS AND THE CAROLINES.
IN CHINAS HUNAN PROVINCE ENCIRCLED CHINESE FORCES WERE FIGHTING
DESPERATELY AT HENGYANG, VITAL RAILWAY JUNCTION IN HUNAN PROVINCE. A CHINESE ARMY SPOKESMAN CHARGED THE JAPANESE WERE USING POISON GAS. AMERICAN AIRMEN WHO LOST THEIR BASE AT HENGYANG CONTINUED THEIR ATTACKS THROUGH THE PROVINCE. IN BURMA CHINESE FORCES LAUNCHED A SOUTHWARD DRIVE FROM CAP-

2 July '44, Associated Press news

TURED MOGAUNG DOWN THE MAIN RAILWAY LEADING TO MANDALAY. CHINESE EXPEDITION-ARY FORCES OUT OF YUNAN PROVINCE DRIVING TOWARD THE BURMA BORDER NARROWED TO 64 MILES THE GAP BETWEEN THEMSELVES AND GENERAL STILWELLS AMERICAN CHINESE SOLDIERS IN THE DRIVE TO FREE THE OLD BURMA ROAD AS A SUPPLY LINE INTO CHINA.

ALLIED SOUTHWEST PACIFIC AIR FORCES CONTINUED TO POUND THE JAP YAP BASE SHOWING THE JAPS HOW BY SHOOTING DOWN THREE JAP PLANES AS LIBER-ATORS UNLOADED 63 TONS OF BOMBS. GENERAL MAC ARTHURS COMMUNIQUE ANNOUNCED TODAY. OTHER NIGHT FLYING LIBERATORS HIT PALAU, SETTING FIRE TO A JAP MERCHANTMAN.

WASHINGTON::::::::::
THE UNITED STATES FINALLY BROKE OFF RELATIONS WITH FINLAND FRIDAY, DECLARING THAT SCANDINAVIAN COUNTRY TO BE A "PUPPET OF NAZI GERMANY." THE AMERICAN GOVERNMENT THROUGH THE STATE DEPARTMENT MADE THE BREAT AT APPROXIMATELY ELEVEN A.M. EASTERN WARTIME SATURDAY. A STATE DEPARTMENT OFFICIAL AT THAT HOUR HANDED TO THE FINNISH CHARGE DE AFFAIRS ALEXANDER THESLESS HIS PASSPORT AND A NOTE FROM SECRETARY HULL GIVING THE REASONS FOR THE BREAK.

SUPREME ALLIED EXPEDITIONARY FORCES::::::::::
THE GERMANS REINFORCED BY TROOPS THROWN INTO ACTION FOR THE FIRST TIME DROVE A ONE MILE WEDGE INTO THE BASE OF THE ALLIED POSITIONS SOUTHWEST OF CAEN FRIDAY BEFORE THE ATTACK MELTED IN A STORM OF ARTILLERY FIRE AND THE BRITISH SWEPT BACK AND WIDENED THEIR SALIENT SWEEP FROM THE SOUTH. WITH THE INITIATIVE STILL FIRMLY IN THE HANDS OF GEN SIR BERNARD MONTGOMERY THE ALLIES THEN STRUCK EAST DIRECTLY TOWARD CAEN AND SOUTH, DEEPENING THE SALIENT BETWEEN THE ODON AND ORNE RIVERS. AN ENEMY BROADCAST REPORTED A CONCENTRA-TION OF THREE BRITISH INFANTRY AND THREE TANK DIVISIONS SOUTHWEST OF CAEN AND SAID "ITCAN BE ASSUMED THAT MONTGOMERY EXPECTS A DECISIVE BREAK THROUGH

HERE " IF SO, THE GERMANS HAVE AT LEAST TWENTY FOUR FEWER TANKS WITH WHICH TO FACE THE ONSLAUGHT, BECAUSE THAT IS WHAT THEIR FUTILE COUNTERATTACKS FROM THE MOUTHWARD NE?R GRANVILLE COST THEM. A DOZEN WERE DESTROYED IN THE ARTILLERY BARRAGE AND THE REST WERE KNOCKED OUT BY ROCKET FIRING FIGHTER PLANES.

ROME::::::::
THE ALLIED MACHINE ROLLED FORWARD FRIDAY NIGHT ON A ONE HUNDRED EIGHT MILE FRONT FROM THE TYRRHENIAN SEA TO BEYOND LAKE TRASIMENO WITH THE BATTERED NAZI FULL FLIGHT BEFORE LT. GEN. MARK CLARKS AMERICANS ON THE EXTREME LEFT WING.

HOLLYWOOD::::::::
A DAUGHTER WAS BORN TODAY TO ACTRESS MAUREEN O'HARA, WIFE OF MARINE LT. WILL PRICE, FORMER FILM DIRECTOR.

BOSTON::::::::
MANUEL ORTIZ, THE WORLDS BANTOM WEIGHT CHAMPION FROM EL CENTRO, CALIFORNIA, FRIDAY CELEBRATED A SUCCESSFUL EASTERN BOXING DEBUT. HE GAINED AN EIGHT ROUND DECISION OVER LARRY BOLVIN OF PROVIDENCE R.I., BEFORE 3299 THRUSDAY NIGHT AT BRAVES FIELD.

CHICAGO::::::::
ALVIN KRAUSE, 29, UNDER SENTENCE TO LIFE IMPRISONMENT FOR MURDER, WAS SENTENCED FRIDAY TO DEATH IN THE ELECTRIC CHAIR FOR A SECOND HOLDUP KILLING. SENTENCE WAS IMPOSED BY JUDGE HAROLD WARD OF CRIMINAL COURT, BEFORE WHON KRAUSE WAS CONVICTED JUNE EIGHTEENTH ON MURDERING WALTER BUST, 65, YEAR OLD MANAGER OF A CURRENCY EXCHANGE ON JUNE 19, 1943.

ST. LOUIS::::::::::

CHESTER LAKE, A FIELD REPRESENTATIVE FOR THE RURAL ELECTRICIFICATION ADMINISTRATION SAID FRIDAY HE "LOST THREE POUNDS" AS A RESULT OF A SELF IMPOSED FAST IN PROTEST OF WHAT HE CALLED "POLITICAL DOMINATION" OF THE AGENCY. HE SAID HE HAD TAKEN NO NOURISHMENT OF ANY KIND SINCE ADDRESSING A LUNCHEON CLUB WEDNESDAY NOON, BUT CONSUMES A GLASS OF WATER EACH HOUR TO PREVENT DEHYDRATION. HE NORMALLY WEIGHS TWO HUNDRED POUNDS, HE SAID.

WASHINGTON::::::::::

PRESIDENT ROOSEVELT FRIDAY APPROVED A ONE YEAR EXTENSION OF THE PRICE CONTROL AND STABILIZATION BOARD AND IN AN ACCOMPANYING SPEECH, HE MILDLY REBUKED CONGRESS FOR RELAXING THE PENALTIES AGAINST PRICE LAW VIOLATIONS.

LONDON::::::::::

MOSCOW ANNOUNCED FRIDAY NIGHT FIFTY THOUSAND GERMANS WERE KILLED AND TWENTY THOUSAND TAKEN CAPTIVE ON THE FIRST WHITE RUSSIAN FRONT BETWEEN JUNE 24 AND 29TH. ON THE SECOND WHITE RUSSIAN FRONT THE RUSSIANS BROADCAST, SAID THIRTY THOUSAND GERMANS WERE KILLED AND 3295 CAPTURED.

A BRITISH PORT::::::::::

THREE TOP RANKING GERMAN OFFICERS CAPTURED AT CHERBOURG, GENERAL SCHLIEBEN AND GENERAL STATTLER AND ADMIRAL HENNECKE WERE BROUGHT TO ENGLAND FRIDAY IN A TANK LANDING SHIP. THEY WERE GIVEN EVERY COURTESY ON THE WAY OVER. EACH HAVING HIS OWN CABIN AND AN ORDERLY AND FREEDOM OF THE WARD ROOM. GENERAL SCHLIEBEN, GIVEN A HAIRCUT, APOLIGIZED BECAUSE HE HAD NO MONEY TO PAY, ASKED THAT HE SHOULD DO, AND FOUND UP SIGNING THE SOLDIERS AUTOGRAPH ALBUM WITH QUOTE THANK YOU VERY MUCH FOR THE HAIRCUT UNQUOTE.

LONDON:::::::::
HITLERS BLIND MAN VENGEANCE SENT BOMBERS DRONING ACROSS SOUTHERN ENGLAND IN DEADLY PROCESSION ALL DAY FRIDAY KILLING A NUMBER OF PEOPLE INCLUDING BABIES IN A RURAL NURSERY HOME. THE SINISTER FLYING BOMBS CAME OVER IN INCREASING NUMBERS BY DAYLIGHT LEAVING DREADFUL SCENES AT WIDELY SCATTERED PLACES BUT NONE WAS SO POIGNANT AS THE DEMOLISHED NURSERY WHERE BEGRIMED RESCUE SQUADS STILL TOILED FRIDAY LOOKING FOR BODIES.

NO MO'

LIEUTENANT GENERAL "SAITO'S" LAST
MESSAGE TO JAPANESE OFFICERS
AND MEN DEFENDING SAIPAN

THIS MESSAGE WAS DELIVERED BY SAITO AT APPROXIMATELY 0800 THE MORNING OF 6 JULY, JUST PRIOR TO THE GENERAL'S DEATH AT 1000 THAT DAY.

MESSAGE TO OFFICERS AND MEN DEFENDING SAIPAN

"I AM ADDRESSING THE OFFICERS AND MEN OF THE IMPERIAL ARMY OF SAIPAN.
FOR MORE THAN TWENTY DAYS SINCE THE AMERICAN DEVILS ATTACKED THE OFFICERS, MEN AND CIVILIAN EMPLOYEES OF THE IMPERIAL ARMY AND NAVY ON THIS ISLAND HAVE FOUGHT WELL AND BRAVELY. EVERYWHERE THEY

HAVE DEMONSTRATED THE HONOR AND GLORY OF THE IMPERIAL FORCES. I EXPECTED THAT EVERY MAN WOULD DO HIS DUTY.

HEAVEN HAS NOT ▓ GIVEN US AN OPPORTUNITY. WE HAVE NOT BEEN ABLE TO UTILIZE FULLY THE TERRAIN. WE HAVE FOUGHT IN UNISON UP TO THE PRESENT TIME, BUT NOW WE HAVE NO MATERIALS WITH WHICH TO FIGHT AND OUR ARTILLERY, FOR ATTACK HAS BEEN COMPLETELY DESTROYED. OUR COMRADES HAVE FALLEN ONE AFTER ANOTHER. DESPITE THE BITTERNESS OF DEFEAT, WE PLEDGE SEVEN LIVES TO REPAY OUR COUNTRY.

THE BARBAROUS ATTACK OF THE ENEMY IS BEING CONTINUED. EVEN THOUGH THE ENEMY HAS OCCUPIED ONLY A CORNER OF SAIPAN WE ARE DYING WITHOUT AVAIL UNDER THE VIOLENT SHELLING AND BOMBING. WHETHER WE ATTACK OR WHETHER WE STAY WHERE WE ARE, THERE IS ONLY DEATH. HOWEVER, IN DEATH THERE IS LIFE. WE MUST UTILIZE THIS OPPORTUNITY TO EXALT TRUE JAPANESE MANHOOD. I WILL ADVANCE WITH THOSE WHO REMAIN TO DELIVER STILL ANOTHER BLOW TO THE AMERICAN DEVILS, AND LEAVE MY BONES ON SAIPAN AS A BULWARK OF THE PACIFIC.

AS IT SAYS IN THE "SENJINKUN" (BATTLE ETHICS), "I WILL NEVER SUFFER THE DISGRACE OF BEING TAKEN ALIVE", AND I WILL OFFER UP THE COURAGE OF MY SOUL AND CALMLY REJOICE IN LIVING BY THE ETERNAL PRINCIPLE.

HERE I PRAY WITH YOU FOR THE ETERNAL LIFE OF THE EMPEROR AND THE WELFARE OF THE COUNTRY AND I ADVANCE TO SEEK OUT THE ENEMY.

"FOLLOW ME"

**"SEVEN LIVES TO REPAY OUR COUNTRY" WAS THE PASSWORD DESIGNATED BY THE BATTALION ORDER (26 JUNE) SETTING THE ATTACK THAT RESULTED IN A BREAKTHROUGH FROM NAFUTAN POINT.

we'll catch up with them on some future invasion. Right now our plans are uncertain, except that we'll be in Oahu for awhile again, loading, provisioning, and getting some minor repairs where needed. This letter won't be mailed until we get there.

We are taking back a load of damaged tanks and thousands of empty shell cases. They surely threw a lot of ammunition at Saipan. We took most of them off destroyers and cruisers. We didn't expend very much ourselves—only in air raids—since we have only 40-millimeter and 20-millimeter guns. The anti-aircraft that does the damage is the 90-millimeter type which warships carry.

I am liking life on our LST more and more. It is rather informal, and we don't have to put up with too many restrictions that usually obtain a ship with commanders aboard. We have a commander in charge of our present small convoy, and he is on the ship ahead. If we get fifty yards off range, he sends messages frantically. So standing a four-hour watch can be pretty tiresome, constantly checking distances and altering speed. Tonight our gyrocompass went out when I was on watch, and the helmsman began taking the ship all over the ocean—since he just follows the compass course. Actually the compass spun around to a 160-degree error. Before we knew it, we were all screwed up. Now we're steering by magnetic. You should have heard the commander! I thought Captain Kittredge would jump out of his skin.

We are traveling in a small group now, but St. Brendan seems to be with us. We had three submarine contacts so far, but an accompanying destroyer dropped depth charges. I think I'll send you a much-prized battle flag. I must go now.

23 July '44

Last night I had one of those evenings that one gets to look forward to after a stretch out here, namely reading a batch of mail. We got into port yesterday afternoon, came steaming, churning, lurching, rolling through the blue into the sapphire and turquoise about the reefs, right through the narrow channel that has probably seen more warships than any other and tied up to a dock which is a stone's throw from a grove of poinciana trees. Small boat over the side—fleet post office—chow in the meantime (liver and onions) then fourteen sacks of mail and everybody

feeling happy. Last mail we had was Eniwetok, two weeks ago, so everybody was rather hungry for news from home. Eighteen letters for this
plyer of the brine calls for a real set-up. So he arranges his pillows, has
the lights adjusted properly, a cigar on his trunk (which serves as a table),
ashtray, matches, and a big glass of torpedo juice. So I spend the evening
reveling in a stack of mail.

It's not that hot out here. Actually the weather is moderate most of
the time. Sometimes in a great calm, things become torrid, but not over
95 and never humid. I think the adjustment period I went through led
me to believe that it was hotter than it really is. In any case weather is no
concern of mine. I like it all. This is the rainy season—July, August—and
almost daily we have had showers. Three days ago we had a 30-mph gale
for nearly 48 hours, with rain like needles. I thought the ship would break
in two or perhaps three. It was nice for a change. I like rain. It's fun to be
on the con with an oilskin and a big sou'wester. The helmsmen really
work in a sea like that. Water over the bow, dishes breaking, food sliding
around in the ice boxes, falling out when you open the doors, sleepy men
rolling out of their bunks. Breaks the monotony.

You asked me about general quarters. It is neither a person nor a
place. It is a condition, which, when prevailing, causes everyone to don
his life jacket (Mae Wests they are called—made in Greenfield), helmet
and pistol and requires that he go to his assigned post, pending possible
action of a militant nature. This means that all guns are manned, and, in
my case, I go up to the conning tower with binoculars and look wise.
When planes come over, the captain screams, "What is it?" and so far I
have been able to tell him. Most of the time we open fire only on orders
of the convoy commander, who has all sorts of devices for determining
whether planes are friendly or not—so that relieves me of the responsibility. But he always wants to know anyway.

Lately I've been thinking (I still do that occasionally) how really difficult it can be for some people to maintain their position in life. Some
officers who find themselves in a position requiring leadership and authority and the ability to command respect find it very burdensome, largely
because they hope that gold on the hat and the help of rules and the
threat of punitive measures will take care of that. It will not. It may produce results for a time, but it will never produce any genuine relation-
ship that will hold water. The problem of the officer and the enlisted man

on a ship is no small one. I know many officers who would gladly resign their commissions simply because they feel they are losing their grip on the men. They made their first mistake by trying to grip them with superficial means instead of leading with intelligent and genuine measures. They say it's a mark of laziness to subscribe to the belief that "it's not what I do that counts, it's what I am," but I think there's a lot of truth in that. I think men or women are foolish not to make use of their advantages and superiorities. It makes their work easier, and people will respect them for their ability to get things done without sweating about it.

If one lives well and does what he thinks is right, he not only commands others' respect and admiration, but he respects himself, which is all important. People who are forever compromising soon lose confidence in themselves. When I die, I want to go down knowing I had my eyes ahead and that I didn't belittle myself in my own eyes—in short, respecting myself. So even if the communists take all my possessions and the bureaucrats take over my house for a vacation lodge because I represented capital, inheritance and a way of life they hoped to obtain but could never hold because they can't wear the mantle any more than a drone can wear a pearl necklace, at least I'll be able to turn towards the block with a clean conscience and the knowledge that they realized I didn't give in or compromise or hedge around—and that here is someone with some mettle.

Hello to all and have a good midsummer.

25 July '44

I'm going to drink some beer tomorrow, and I'm going to spend the day in leisure, probably at Waikiki. Maybe I'll have dinner with the Red Cross girl I met on the train: Marjorie Dellangelo, from Akron, Ohio—if I can get in touch with her. Or go tea dancing with Mitsui Kotma, the Chinese girl I met through the army officers. At any rate, I'm going to get a change of scene and just do what I want for a change.

Pearl Harbor is a beautiful place in some respects. There's a rainbow every evening. Then all the masthead lights of all the ships go on and reflect in the harbor, the moon comes up, and peace descends on a scene that could pack all kinds of wallops. This nearly happened the first night we got in. There was an alarm at two in the morning—unknown vessels 150 miles off. Scuttlebutt has it that a Japanese task force was about to release planes on Pearl Harbor, but I think that is unfounded. However, the alert did last until the following noon.

The day I was in the hospital after getting a bump on the head, a terrific explosion took place, which might have involved me if I hadn't been in the hospital. I saw a clipping in the paper from the States—just a brief notice—but actually it was lots worse than the one that lately occurred in San Francisco. Seven LSTs loaded with all kinds of things, mostly ammunition and high-test gasoline, blew up, killing hundreds of men and wounding nearly a thousand. Our ship was a hundred yards away, the deck was showered with debris, but it was moved out of the harbor without serious damage or injury. Only injury occurred to a radar man from Columbus, Ohio, who is married to a girl from Evanston. It was the worst tragedy in Hawaii since December 7, 1941. Ships all loaded with materiel and soldiers—ready to move out.

We are moored next to a coral bank, which is covered with a grove of poinciana trees. Turtledoves flit about and sing their love songs all day. I like Hawaii better this time.

The liberty boat just returned with a load of happy sailors. The crew is divided into port and starboard sections. One section has liberty one day, the other the next. It was the first liberty for these men in many weeks, and the general impression is that they made the most of it in no uncertain terms.

They all came back with leis around their necks, their once-clean whites dirty, their arms loaded with trinkets. Trying to climb up the Jacob's ladder in this condition provides some good laughs. Some of the men had been promoted in their ranks, and they usually pass around cigars on those occasions. So I did quite well because they know I like cigars.

One-hundred four men, and each one different and interesting in his own way. After a big day ashore they'll all be hungry, so about nine thirty we'll have some snacks —ham, boiled shrimp, fruit, cold roast beef, coffee. We got some excellent honeydew melon today, about as good as any I've had. Nice to get some fresh fruit again. We were all out of fresh things when we arrived here.

I'm going to send a box of things, and in it will be some things for you if you want them. I sent the troop guidon I found, and I hope it

arrives safely for it's my prized souvenir. I don't know whether the kimono I got is linen or raw silk, but I think it's the latter. I do hope the little
bowls don't break, but they probably will. I'm cutting off the breech end
of some large shells, which might possibly make ashtrays if they are ma-
chined down and polished. If Charles has a grinder and buffer, perhaps
he could finish them off. However, all this, which means something to
me, will probably be so much junk to anyone else.

I'll be thinking of you tomorrow when I'm on the beach. Wish you
could be here to enjoy it. Good night and much love.

1 August '44

August already—the sunny maturing month—ironweed, purple
moon, locusts.

A mine recoverer has been tied alongside the last few days. The skipper is from Swarthmore, so we've had several chatty moments. He runs a
very scholarly ship and has all nine officers doing all sorts of things. They
are forever sending semaphore messages, instead of simply saying things,
and blinking flashlights at each other. In spite of this beaver behavior,
they are mostly a good lot. I have been with them to the movies a few
times in a nice little club just a few hundred yards from here. The only
reason I go is that while the movie grinds on, one can drink Champagne
Velvet beer, made in Terre Haute, Indiana, and smoke White Owls, all the
while comfortably mounted in leather chairs. The other night I saw *The
Bridge of San Luis Rey* mostly through the bottom of a glass, which I
think helped the effect, especially the dramatic bridge-breaking episode.
These few visits to the cinema have served to renew my determination
never to endure a motion picture without the necessities of life at hand
and have helped me to recall the pleasure I had in seeing *Gone with the
Wind* on a Tuesday morning with four U.C. students fortified with beer
and sandwiches.

Friday is Coast Guard Day, so we're having a special dinner at seven
o'clock and if possible, a band concert by some borrowed band in the
locality. Special dinner will probably be shrimp cocktail, onion soup, fried
chicken, fresh peas, potatoes, slaw, hot rolls, fresh pineapple, ice cream
and coffee.

Well, I must get some sleep. I hope the August nights won't be too cool, or are you ready for cool weather after all the heat? Good night. I love you.

```
CV22/

                    U. S. S. INDEPENDENCE




        SUNDAY........13 August, 1944


        YOU ARE CORDIALLY INVITED

            TO ATTEND

        DIVINE SERVICES ABOARD SHIP...USS INDEPENDENCE

        0900      CATHOLIC MASS.....HANGAR DECK.....Chaplain Kelly
                  (preceded by Confessions in Library)

        1000      PROTESTANT SERVICES.....HANGAR DECK..Chap. O'Connor



                        D. F. Kelly
                        Lt. Cmdr. (ChC) USN
```

Invitation to divine services aboard USS *Independence*

14 August '44

We have been having a busy week here in Honolulu. Last Saturday, 5 August, the day after our CG Day celebration, Captain Kittredge was relieved. I think he's going back to civilian life, having served his time. He was replaced by our executive officer, Lieutenant Gershon. Captain Kittredge's leave taking was according to protocol—general muster, a few words to the crew, reading of his orders relieving him, the succeeding command reading his orders placing him in command, then over the side with a waiting small boat.

The new skipper hasn't had any more experience than I have had at sea. I really have more because he never cons the ship or stands watches (executive officers don't, except on very small vessels), but he has the good sense to entrust some duties to the other officers and is not afraid of things happening to him or the ship, which is very smart of him. Therefore, we all feel we have some part in the ship's organization now to a greater extent than before. For example, if the ship has to be moved from one anchorage to another, he knows we can do it, and he himself leaves the ship for some fun. Kittredge never left the ship unless for dire necessity.

Last Sunday, August 6, I went to the other side of the island with Mrs. Helen Suironton and her boyfriend, Major Herman. Mrs. Suironton is a Korean whose husband, now dead, was once an officer in the navy. She is a very hospitable person. I sent our steward out to her house with a gallon of real soy sauce, and now she can't get enough. It's to them what real olive oil is to the Italians.

On the other side of the island live her parents, Mr. and Mrs. Chong. They have a simple farm on a gently rising slope from the beach. That is the windward side of the island, and the surf is heavy and pounding, throwing its white spume out of its blue bosom. Then the lovely greens—tender warm greens of cane fields, taro patches, mangrove; and the simple wooden house—one floor, the ample kitchen,

Change of Command—*LST 169* Captain Kittredge turns over command to Lieutenant Gershon.

Mrs. Suironton

the well-stocked larder, and American refrigerator, oil lamps, bare floors—the typically ephemeral oriental house (the soul only is eternal—no need to build stone dwellings), the goats, chickens, and mother and father—venerable, honest, happy to see daughter (no English except "hello" [alo] and "good-bye"), happy, smiling, kind, hospitable. Scads of people, other sons and daughters and their broods of smiling almond-eyed rays of sun, hide and seek with the kids, Ronnie, nephew of nine has a birthday, so I made the mistake of giving him a dollar, and that was enough for all the children—such displays of affection. Then the perpetual dinner: sit when you want to and eat, eat, with chop sticks (I became very proficient)—chicken, steak, cucumber, rice, shrimp, soup, salads, avocado, nuts, seaweed, whiskey, rum, sake, tea, biscuits—a feast indeed.

The ride over the Pali pass, where Kamehameha threw the enemy over the cliff and established monarchical supremacy once and for all, was marked by the magnificent tropical scenery, volcanic heights, poinciana, palm, vines of all kinds, waterfalls, perpetual rainbows, peasants, townsfolk.

During the week: work on the ship, provisions aboard, tons of food for the next cruise, getting the galley painted, cleaning the wardroom. I'm mess treasurer this month and have charge of the stewards, who are always willing to eat and loaf, but sometimes slow in cleaning rooms, swabbing the decks, pressing clothes and changing the sheets, not to mention that they need jacking up about serving at table and serving *hot* coffee instead of warm. I have them pretty well lined up. Restricted them for a few liberties because of laziness, and now all is better—*and* the coffee is hot, and when I am awakened in the morning, there is a cup of hot coffee to go with it.

President Roosevelt was hereabouts not long ago. Good campaigner. We were issued cards requesting ballots for the forthcoming presidential election.

Saturday I went ashore—stopped in at the Coast Guard with shipmate Ensign Andris. Called Helen, and she and the major and still another Oriental belle appeared. Back to her house and had a fine dinner, heavily garlicked. Eventually everyone began to doze off, so we just stayed there, in available beds, on couches, on the floor. A big bugle on legs (rooster) awakened us, and after a brief breakfast and an eye opener of 120-proof rum we all went to the cathedral and listened to a Belgian priest expound on the deplorable custom of too much frivolity at weddings.

Then Andris from Philadelphia and I had our hair cut, got a shave, shampoo, mud pack, massage, etc., etc. and back to the CG officer's club for continuance of the recreation.

Soon Helen and the Major appeared, and we had singing and so forth. First time I played the piano since April. Then some more of the officers who were at Helen's the night before appeared, and we were off again, this time to a Chinese restaurant. Back to the ship by ten o'clock, and this morning, back to the provisioning and painting. Helen says she is going to write you and send you her picture with her daughter. She is really a grand person. Also the Red Cross friend, who so kindly banks part of my pay for me (so I won't surrender it to highwaymen) says she is going to write you. It seems part of a plan to keep mothers informed about their sons. At any rate, I think it's a nice gesture. You can be assured I'm being well cared for and happy and getting plenty of recreation.

Really, I'm very happy on this ship. Most of the men are a pretty high calibre. So far I've had practically no disciplinary problems, and I hope I never do.

I'm enclosing a picture of one of the cooks named Leroy Turton, who is delighted that I think he looks like Tyrone Power. What do you think? He is from Buffalo and other places.

I sent a box of souvenirs, which may or may not reach you. In any case, there is a robe which you or Virginia or the waitress at Wong Yie's may desire, a map for Caroline E., a soldier coat and belt for Stephen Rush, ash trays for you all however you all do it. Throw it all out if it doesn't appeal.

Take care of yourself, and my best to Eddie, Virginia and Charles. All my love to you.

Leroy Turton, a cook
on the *LST 169*

21 August '44

We've been here a month now, and I have the feeling that all of us have had a good share of rest and recreation. We are still busy getting the necessary work accomplished, and the decks swarm with welders, paint chippers, ship fitters, and a motley assortment of sailors, Hawaiian workers and typical shipyard loafers. I now have the additional job of supply, which means securing everything that we need in addition to the commissary. But we have a good storekeeper, and I don't have to worry. Furthermore, I have maintained my position as the "executive type," which solves a lot of things. A supply officer should have a desk, and the skipper wants one in my room, but I refuse because that would mean a lot of papers and endless piling up. I do most of my work from the sack. The storekeeper, the steward, the bread cook come in every morning for instructions and with reports of their progress. They really appreciate the confidence I put in them, and they do a better job because of that. Mr. Rosen, the supply officer before me, thought he was running his own business and watched everything like a hawk. However, since one must sleep, he couldn't watch all the time, and they made a point of fouling him up simply because they felt he didn't trust them. I don't care if somebody steals a dozen oranges. One can eat just so much, and you can't sell it on the outside when you're on a ship. Partly for that reason I like sea duty. You don't have that constant finagling that goes on at a shore station and the resulting jealousies. At present, we have what I believe is a very harmonious ship. We have three new officers who are very pleasant fellows, and it is such a relief to have a skipper who puts faith in our abilities and will to do things. Everyone as a result is working better than before—and getting things done faster—and as a result getting more liberty.

There seems to be an officer's club in every stray clump of palm trees here in Honolulu—which makes it nice. I see pretty much of the Red Cross girl, Marjorie Dellangelo, and of the Koreans, and a Chinese girl named Elsie Fong. We go swimming, have cocktails, then have dinner—and much hilarity with it all. Yesterday I spent at Waikiki with Mrs. Suironton. Loveliest sunset I have ever seen—palm trees, surf, purples, oranges, blues—and the general atmosphere of easy goingness—soft climate, soft air.

The other night I went to a luau at Halekai, which is a suburb of Honolulu. We had everything possible to eat and drink, and much fun—much singing and casual lying around on the grass. A luau is a large-scale picnic that is apt to go on for days. Poi is served—eaten with the fingers.

Royal Hawaiian

Waikiki

28 August '44

Honolulu continues to reveal more and more of interest, and I soon will become enamored of it as I do of almost all the places I go.

Let's talk of food now: Leroy Turton, the Tyrone Power of my little galley group, is indeed susceptible to flattery and has lately done a marvelous job of getting fresh island-raised fruits and vegetables: Chinese cabbage, taro root, pineapple, Hawaiian turnips, onions, and tomatoes, the latter of which are hard to get out here. Our ice-boxes are jam-packed and we're more or less ready to go. Tomorrow we take aboard 200 cases of Pepsi Cola. We already have 100 cases of beer. When we're in the down unders, I'll turn bootlegger and sell the stuff to thirsty marines for a dollar a can.

Isidio Idencio, the Philippino lover (he has a girl on the island to whose establishment he manages to escape almost every night, with much oriental subterfuge and innocent rolling of eyes) is, in addition to being a famous lover and poker player, a very good cook when he wants to be, and since he wants to be if I want him to, he cooks some delightful oriental meals, which would make Wong Yie and the so-called better restaurants of Chinese origin hang their ignominious heads in a welter of ancestral shame. He is forever bringing back an armload of rare spices and flavors, and after a little magic and much stewing around, he produces delightful concoctions.

Isidio is a character you would enjoy. He has been in the service for years and was once the fly-weight wrestling champ of the fleet. He is very solicitous about my appearance and seems to enjoy catering to my whims. He presses my clothes and darns my socks and sees that I have ice when I want it and clean towels and that my bed is made without a wrinkle. If I seem displeased with him he becomes sad and manages to let me know through other people (usually Turton) that he is very unhappy, and won't I please reinstate him in my good graces. I guess what he actually fears is that his nocturnal experiences would be somewhat curtailed if I started bearing down on him.

Yesterday, I had lunch at Dillingham's whose fabulous villa makes any of Pliny's establishments look like a gardener's cottage. Twelve people, at three tables, on a terrace of much magnificence, cool breezes, arbors, flowers, Japanese servants in native costumes, musicians with twangy instruments. Delicious roast beef, salad, and a variety of apéritifs, high balls, low balls, whiskey, rum, beer, wine—and pleasant conversation. Mrs. Dillingham is a hostess of rare and magnificent cut.

One of the guests was Admiral [William] Halsey, who, like most big men, was perhaps the easiest conversationalist of all. You might inform Herbert that Admiral Halsey enjoyed my latest version of Villa-Lobos' "Santos Suite." It was the first time I've touched the piano since April, and the dexterity of my fingers was something to behold and probably attributable either to my days with Herschel and his digital tortures or to the pineapple whiskey in the cocktails. At any rate, we all had a good time, and when things began to cool off, I cooled off further by taking a swim in the sapphire pool on still another terrace and followed my exercise by taking a delightful nap under the pomegranate trees that surround the pool. If you want to have an experience, try waking up with an Hawaiian sunset trickling through the pomegranates and hearing the thin plaintive notes of a Japanese melody sifting through the Cambrian vines. What a day. Entertainment at the Dillingham's is informal and restful. After the conventional hour or so after dinner, the guests are turned loose to their wishes—tennis, swimming, sleeping, bowling on the green, pianoing, drinking, cards. Departure is facilitated by the impeccable courtesy of the Japanese butler, who could easily have been the emperor's slave. He calls your car. He packs your swimming suit and urges your return in the name of Madame who has whisked off in a blaze of athletic glory to play tennis about three o'clock. Only six of us had stayed on, and we were given to understand we could stay all night if we desired to.

I'm enclosing a picture of my coconut-minded friend, Peluso, who is a yeoman of the first water and something of a brain about lots of things. Please don't think I enclose it because of the flattering nature of the message on the reverse side. Rather it is for safekeeping.

Also a picture of myself, which the new photographer on board "snapped" with much taking of stances. We now have a combat photographer and a combat artist. Both are good. Raphael de Burgos, the artist, is a source of joy to me. He's promised to do a pen sketch for you of something typical. He's more than an illustrator—he has a point of view—and really he is the top of the artists' milk bottle.

Can Charles grind the shells so that the edges are smooth?

A. G. Peluso

Message on back of photo

To a philosophical shipmate – and best liked officer in the Coast Guard. Being a friend of J J Fern is a high honor

Peluso

J. J. Fern

SUNDAY

****

OLIVER HAZARD PERRY DAY 10 SEPTEMBER, 1944   *****   U.S.S. LST 169

- * - M E N U - * -
--oOo--

DINNER: 1200

ANTI * PASTO

CHICKEN SOUP MINESTRONE

ROAST CHICKEN

DRESSING - GIBLET GRAVY

MASHED SWEET POTATOES - BROWN SYRUP

GREEN PEAS

TOMATO SALAD FRENCH DRESSING

SPONGE CAKE   ICE CREAM

ICED COFFEE MILK-SHAKE

ON 10 SEPTEMBER, 1813, COMMODORE OLIVER HAZARD PERRY DEFEATED THE BRITISH IN
THE BATTLE OF LAKE ERIE. SONS OF SEMPER PARATUS ARE PLEASED TO HONOR THE
MEMORY OF A MAN OF INDOMITABLE COURAGE.
                    "WE HAVE MET THE ENEMY AND THEY ARE OURS."

****

Lieutenant Fern adds a theme to his dinner menu

13 September '44

I guess you've heard it said that when tourists leave Honolulu, they want to jump ship and go back. I can understand that now. What I said before about Hawaii in comparison to the West Indies still holds, but there are, must be, other compensating elements because here is one jomo who hated to see the green-brown hills of Oahu—Diamond Head, Koko Head, Punchbowl, and the Aloha tower at Honolulu harbor—and even the entrance buoys and the control towers fade into misty silhouettes and disappear. It's good to be at sea again, to hear the waves sloshing against the ship and to feel the flung spray of this oh-so-blue water cling to your face, but there was hardly a man aboard who didn't lean on the rail, uncommunicative, with his own thoughts and hate to see the place that we've come to love go out of our lives, for a time at least. The West Indies have friendliness, culture and artistic achievements. Hawaii has friendliness after you get to know the people—only a crude utilitarian culture and no artistic achievements. The attraction lies in falling into the atmosphere of the true Polynesian Hawaii, whose motto is to relax and enjoy. Nature, soft music, palm trees in the moonlight, loving, dancing—slow easy dancing—no rhumbas or anything energetic—drinking, eating pineapple, luaus (elaborate picnics), sleep, bare feet, bathing, the beaches, the fresh surf, oriental food, pineapple swipe, avocados, taro, Chinese cabbage, Japanese shrimp and beer, island gin and pineapple juice, walking around on bare feet on rattan mats, flowers in every female's hair, ginger blossoms ever so fragrant, bougainvillea, hibiscus, pomegranate trees, flying fish, coral—and underneath all the current commercialism, a kind of genuine hospitality that is primitive and ineffaceable.

Sunday we had our last luau. We had been to the beach for a wonderful swim—way out where the surf riders whiz by at forty miles an hour—sun, sleep under the palms, turkey dinner at the club for officers, then back to the Napua for more relaxing, and when my car came for me at midnight, I think you can see why I wasn't particularly anxious to leave or why, next day, as the hills of Oahu faded out of sight, I didn't feel like Balboa in the way of enthusiasm. Not that I'm not glad to be at sea, but I merely tell you these things by way of explaining how one can become enamored of a place if he tries to get out of it what it can offer. Of course it's easy for a man in my position to get around. Lots of men and most women would stay here for six months before they began having a good time, and maybe they wouldn't even then.

Give my best to everyone. Aloha.

Diamond Head

Slow easy dancing

The easy surf

Natives enjoying the surf

Palm trees in the sunset

25 September '44

It's been two weeks since I've written you, or had any mail, because we've been underway. Only today did we reach our "staging point" (same as last time), and I think we'll shove from here tomorrow. I rather regretted leaving Honolulu because I was having such a good time there, but, on the other hand, it is good to get to sea once more. I thought we'd have some rough weather and rolling and pitching, but after the first day the Pacific began living up to its name and has remained so ever since. We have great periods of calm and intense heat. Yesterday we passed through the doldrums, and it seemed everyone was passed out because Sunday is quiet anyhow—all hands knock off except the watch standers.

You should see my room. I think it is now the nicest on the ship—and all my own. I had it painted. We have a new chief boatswain's mate who is an old-timer and really good. He does everything to please me. When we were in Pearl Harbor, I casually mentioned that I wish I had a porthole in my room. By the next morning he had procured welders from the shipyard, a porthole from the old battle ship *Tennessee* (one of those all but destroyed in the bombing), and since then I have had light. At sunset the coxswain of the watch comes in and closes it, and at sunrise he comes in and opens it. My room is now done in a lovely shade of gray green (glossy!) and the bunks and shelves are all the same—making it very svelte. The deck is a bright green, and he is currently making a cocoa palm mat, so I can pad around in my bare feet. He has had my curtain (at the door) bleached and scrubbed till it's as white as the top of the waves on Koko Head's rocks, and he has put furniture polish on my trunk. Idencio has pressed all my clothes, moth-sprayed my winter things and encased them in a sheet—and now I'm all ready for the winter, which I think will be rather equatorial.

Once again we've come out in a mighty convoy, but we don't know yet where we are going. We knew—but those plans were cancelled en route. We are carrying eight army officers and 175 men and all their equipment. As usual they are draped all over the deck. Artillery too. Not quite up to the last crowd—National Guard and naturally much superior, in my opinion. There is an infantry captain, a physician, aboard. He and I have a lot of fun. He is 29, Dave Morris, Oregon, Catholic, rifle expert, spent two years at Heidelberg as a German government scholar. He has lots of experiences to relate.

I hope you are feeling well. I think about you all the time and hope your health and spirits are good. I guess September and its song are all about in Cincinnati. Of course, there's no feeling of fall in the air here. Only water, water, water, atolls, palms, sand, coral and gorgeous sunrises and sunsets, moonlight, sun, rain squalls, flying fish, a laugh a minute, bickerings which I shed off with a shrug and a yawn, and all in all a good feeling. Today I had two wonderful swims. We lowered the ramp, and everybody went hog wild for the refreshing swim. I swam constantly for an hour and feel better than ever.

I am writing this in the dry provision room, which is next to the galley. I remodeled it, had a bulkhead cut out, two ports put in and a kind of bookkeeper's desk installed. Here I sample food, watch over my crazy cooks and occasionally assemble some friends for a fruit juice and the best GI alcohol, which is sometimes used for sterilizing.

We are provisioning again—five tons of food. An LCM just came alongside with halves of mutton, turkey, beef, fish, chicken, ham, sausage and lots of other things.

I guess this will be the last letter for awhile—so don't worry. We can only send mail when we have the opportunity, and from now on, opportunities will probably be rare.

Please take care of yourself, and don't work too hard. I love you.

6 October '44

October already! Hardly seems possible. I received your letter of the 21st and 18th just yesterday—first mail call since we left our first "staging area." Now we are at an advanced base that was taken only last May. How they build things in a hurry! I went ashore the first day and, for the first time in my life, wandered through the dense jungle. Beautiful palms of all kind, eucalyptus, mangrove, vines, birds of brilliant plumage, soft damp earth, lizards, black natives with fuzzy high hairdos. Everything green and lusciously growing, white beaches, more blue water and white surf, outrigger canoes, silent jungle trails, strange noises. Although it was midday and hot in the sun, in the jungle there is quietude and mysterious silent coolness. There are several islands in this group, and the largest is about fifteen miles long and truly a paradise.

Since May the Seabees have swarmed ashore and put up dozens of Quonset huts, chow halls, warehouses, repair shops, post office, chapel, barracks, tents, canteens, and the inevitable officer's club. This last is quite large and intended to accommodate about two thousand men, ostensibly in need of recreation. The only place I've ever been where they must have full commanders acting as shore patrol! Here they had, in the midst of the palms and tropic vines, quantities of whiskey and mountains of beer, including Iron City from Pittsburgh, Griesedieck's from Saint Louis, and Hudepohl from Cincinnati!

Last Sunday we crossed the equator and had a *big* time in front of Neptune Rex. Dale, a chief signalman of long standing, arranged the whole thing, and it was really a big job. Most of the pollywogs were terrified, and nobody slept the night before. Two of the more recalcitrant members had to be chained to the rail all night. The event lasted from 9 AM to 3 PM and included some fines ranging from 1 cent to $25 haircuts by the royal barber, dunkings, a trip through a fifteen-foot ventilator lined with grease and foul-smelling garbage with a fire hose for a pusher, medicine of dubious ingredients, much paddling, stripping and painting and all the rest of the shenanigans that go with such an initiation. Some of the officers who are not too popular with the crew were unmercifully flogged.

Things are really humming around here. We're taking on more supplies every day, and soon we'll be ready for the big deal. Meantime we have all the fun we can—shore parties to pretty little islands with beer and sandwiches for the enlisted men. We're going to take on 200 more soldiers, and Lord knows where we'll put them.

We aren't allowed to go swimming from the ship (only from beaches) on account of sharks and other denizens of the deep. Oddly enough, the climate down here is very pleasant. It is hot, of course, but not too bad, and there is always a pleasant breeze.

There are lots of British around, and since this is a British island, the traffic is on the left. I guess they are waiting for the day they can haul down the American flag and hoist the livery jack. Smart people—the British.

I had the best dinner today. Thick tender steak and avocado salad followed by a few cool beers. Life aboard here could be lots worse.

Today I heard "Fantasie Impromptu" over the radio. It reminded me so of you at the piano. Well, I must be thinking about retiring to my pastel boudoir. Take care of yourself and say hello to all.

8 October '44

This morning we went to Mass on an aircraft carrier. The chaplain service everywhere is remarkable, although I'm sure it's only because the chaplains work so tirelessly. Last night one came aboard our ship—a Benedictine, young and friendly, and I made confession to him. We also had Holy Communion this morning. We also got paid today from the disbursing officer aboard another ship. So now I have lots of money and nothing to do with it. I don't gamble. Lots of the men are always gambling. Chief Dale was just in and told me he won $440 in twenty minutes a while ago. Tonight there are movies on a nearby ship. I hardly ever go to the movies. I'd rather read and drink some of my Ballantines. I have three books going at once: *Blessed Are the Meek, The Late George Apley,* and *The Island of Desire,* the latter of which is by a person who gave up U.S. civilization and lived on a South Sea island. His name is Frisbie, and it is published (1944) by Doubleday Doran.

I guess things are beginning to perk generally in the Middle West. Did you get any new clothes for the fall? I can hardly believe it's so late in the year. Last year this time I was settling down into a season of hunting and having a good time around Philadelphia. How we change locale. I hope we get to China or some exotic place. Even Australia. I doubt it though. But then you can never tell what they'll dream up. I am pretty happy aboard this ship in spite of the inevitable difficulties. I thank my stars for a few years in the National Guard every day.

Well, I must get to my duties around the galley. Today we had the best tenderloin. In a little while we're going to have cheese and beer. Oh boy.

Lieutenant (jg) Fern on *LST 169,* October 1944

1 November '44—All Saints' Day

It has been several weeks since I have written you—and of course some time since I have heard from you—and I am wondering how you are. I hope you are well and thriving and that the middle of autumn finds you and Cincinnati and the family and your circle of friends and acquaintances in a mellow mood.

My last letter to you was posted from the Admiralty Islands—Manus, to be exact. It seems that the powers that be decided to leave Yap alone for the time and proceed to the Philippines, so our plans were changed during our week's layover at Manus, and we took on more men and more supplies and steamed in a mighty convoy to Leyte, which, if you will look at the chart, is a fairly central island of the Philippine group. Changed plans involved taking on more troops, so then we had artillery, Seabees, infantry, engineers, and quarter-masters, including a few navy and Coast Guards for the invasion work. We had a rather spirited time, socially, with all these people aboard. While the thirty-odd officers crowded us somewhat, still the pleasure of their company more than outweighed any discomfort their presence, with all their gear, entailed.

We in the commissary department rather outdid ourselves, I think, and made every effort to maintain our boast that the *169* has the best chow in the Pacific. I am enclosing a menu, which sounds more imposing than it actually turned out to be, since it is merely a translation in a Manila dialect of a rather simple roast beef dinner. The ambrosia touch you will recognize as my particular contribution, and I might say that I have managed to convince some pastry-enamored people that it is the fitting close to a heavy meal.

Idencio, the steward, was elated at the thought of going to the Philippines, for his parents and family are still in Manila; consequently, he has been stirring about with some sense of authority and striving to please everyone at the same time. He has a way of fixing steak with a slight tinge of garlic that would make the most indifferent eater scream with delight. Two Polish army cooks were forever begging to make geroumke and pierugo (chopped meat rolled in cabbage leaves with hot sauce and small cakes). Ries, the imbibing cook, blossomed out with pineapple upside-down cake and fresh raspberry shortcake. (This last culinary success

U.S.S. LST 169

WARDROOM MESS

EN ROUTE: ADMIRALTY ISLANDS TO PHILIPPINES

- INVASION EVE -
OCTOBER 19, 1944

S U P P E R

HIPPON COCTEL

SINGANG NO SOPAS

ACEITUNA   APIO

INIHAW NA CARNE CON SARSA

DUROG NA PATATAS CON LECHE

VERDENG PEAS AT MANTIKILLA

REPOLLO NA ENSALADO

AMBROSIA

BIBINGCA NA CHOCOLATE

CAFE

Menu by Lieutenant Fern (with the aid of Idencio, no doubt)

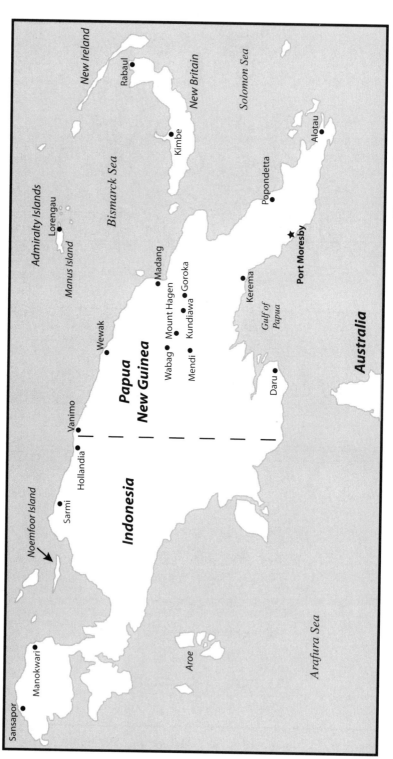

Map supplied by author; drawn by Jim Robinson

prompted a celebration on his part, which ended disastrously. He managed to get some of the sick bay's sterilizing alcohol and go charging about the decks like a berserk bull. So he was demoted to ship's cook second class and fined $80, which I thought was a bit rough because actually he's harmless and a hard worker.) Peluso, the Italian yeoman, made pizza (tomato and cheese pie), and Umdenstock, an army baker, made apple popovers as if possessed. The army officers came aboard with thirty cases of beer, and each of them had quarts of whiskey tucked away in his bed roll. So you can imagine that even though there was something in the atmosphere of a final feast (of eight days), there was also a healthy measure of unmitigated gayety and good fellowship. Times like these one will never forget, and they come under the heading of the compensations of military life.

I had the dawn watch when we steamed into San Pedro Bay. Shortly after four o'clock the big guns of battleships and cruisers began sending their red tracers onto a beach we could not yet see. The water was millpond quiet, and in the warm dawn there was a feeling that we were being watched and that our movements were being relayed by a net of radio operators, runners, messengers. Then came that sweetish odor of death, which I came to know so well at Saipan. The bombers that had hit the island during previous days had taken a toll, and the soft Philippine breeze carried that information to us. A morning star hung down, a streak of pale light showed in the East, and for the life of me all I could think of, with that odor, was Bach's "Come Sweet Death." The shores and mountains of Leyte soon became visible. We could see Dinagat Island on our left, Homonhon dead ahead, and Leyte just off the port bow. Even with the shelling, which was spasmodic, a clammy quiet prevailed. Daybreak revealed hundreds of ships—battleships, cruisers, destroyers, LSTs, LSDs, LCMs, LCVPs, LSRs, LCIs, LCTs, transports, cargo ships, oilers, tugs, freighters, aircraft carriers, tenders, lighters—everything the navy has. By nine o'clock we had taken our beaching formation, and the line ships were plastering the beach with terrific roars. All the soldiers aboard were dressed and garbed with their fifty pounds of rifles, carbines, pistols, blankets, shelter-halves, mess-kits, K rations, ammunition, knives, hatchets, shovels. They had had steak and eggs for breakfast to last them for a long day, and when they climbed into the amphibious tanks, each one was given a sandwich and two apples.

Promptly at ten o'clock we turned our noses to the beach, lowered the ramps five hundred yards from shore, and out rolled hundreds of tanks for a distance of two miles. At the same time the LCIs and destroyers poured thousands of rockets on a strip of beach two miles long and 1,000 yards deep. By the time the tanks reached the beach, there was scarcely a tree left standing, and, as a result, very unlike Saipan, the beachhead was taken with no resistance from the enemy outside of a very few mortar shells.

An hour later we moved up to the beach and began unloading the non-amphibious vehicles and tons of supplies. So I girded myself and went ashore in a DUKW and went a mile inland to where some of our infantry was supposed to be. I found them all right, about three o'clock, digging foxholes and preparing for the night. They had accomplished their initial objective way ahead of schedule. So I visited here and there, then went to the artillery positions and the engineers' dugouts and wound up with a visit to the division headquarters that was set up in what was left of a Catholic church. The village of Dulag was completely destroyed, and this church was the only building still recognizable as such. Everything else was built of bamboo and thatch, so there wasn't too much of a problem to level them. The natives, who are supposed to be friendly, had evacuated to the hills, and only a few who were too lazy to move were killed or injured. I wonder if they appreciate being "liberated" in this manner. At any rate, we had gained an excellent foothold in distinct contrast to the flimsy, deadly and costly toehold that our troops barely held at Saipan. But the ever-present snipers were still around—in holes, in trees. I realized this when I heard the easily recognized Japanese machine-gun fire and saw bullets go ricocheting off the church's walls. It was getting dark, so I started back to the ship.

Dulag was no more. Now it was a seething mass of men and machinery—anti-aircraft weapons, trucks, supply dumps, aid stations, bulldozers, communications riggers. A few chickens and pigs roamed forlornly about the ruins of their owners' houses; three indifferent water buffalos stood in the midst of wreckage, swishing their tails and chewing their cuds; swarms of skinny natives were being rounded up in compounds for the night; wounded soldiers from the front were being carted into the dressing stations; every soldier was digging a foxhole. It was nearly dark when I returned to where our ship lay with its great jaws plopped on the sand. Bulldozers were still pushing sand up to the ramp to provide a more solid exit. So I sat down beside a tank and talked with a soldier. This was his fifth invasion, and he seemed inured to it all and prepared for months of discomfort. I began to realize what he would be facing. As soon as darkness fell, swarms of insects came charging out of the swamps that comprise most of Leyte Valley. Sand crabs filled his foxhole, then it began to rain, to pour, and the exhausting heat of the day was changed to chilling dampness. It actually became cold. The insects were biting unmercifully. What those soldiers face! Months in a malarial, choleric climate. (I have taken shots for cholera and malaria. This plus my tetanus, typhoid, scarlet fever inoculations should make me impregnable.) When I returned to the ship, a crescent moon was struggling to appear through the clouds, and the western sky was blazing in oriental glory just as it always had. The cross atop the church was still untouched and looked down on this scene with a timeless gaze.

That night began the first of a series of 32 air raids, which we had during the next seven days and nights. We were at General Quarters 43 times, and on two occasions for over 20 hours each. There was plenty of excitement for all of us and several hair-raising moments when the Japanese Vals and Bettys and Irvings dove on us. Our ship managed to shoot down two planes and get hits in two others. That is pretty good, considering that we don't have too much ordnance and the largest gun is a forty-millimeter.

The second day was the first time I have seen an air attack. Four Japanese Vals came out of the sun at noon and swooped down. One of them crashed a few hundred yards from our stern, another on the beach close by. That night the ammunition dump on the beach was hit by a bomb dropped from a high lever, and we watched the terrific conflagration all night. We withdrew from the beach because of the flying shrapnel and anchored about six hundred yards offshore. We estimated that a three weeks' supply for a regiment went up in flames: rockets and star shells and the big stuff of the artillery, along with countless drums of gasoline, exploding all night. Hundreds of soldiers bivouacked nearby were killed, and next day we had several who survived come aboard for treatment and clothing.

Next day we and two other LSTs were designated to remain in the area to unload remaining cargo ships, and the rest of the convoy steamed out. This left us pretty much alone, and that night in the light of a half moon, two big Japanese bombers came out of a cloud and nearly hit our mast. We shot one of them, and it crashed with a roar and burned for three hours. By the fifth night some fighter planes, P38s, appeared on the scene, and we saw some pretty exciting dogfights with Japanese fighters. But as soon as darkness came on, the fighters grounded, and the bombers came over again. The anti-aircraft fire that was thrown up from all parts of the harbor was certainly a sight.

While we were carrying on in this manner, the Japanese fleet—four battle ships, five cruisers, and seven destroyers—steamed up to the mouth of the harbor, threatening to bottle us in. Fortunately for us, a few of our destroyers on patrol managed to intercept them. They met disaster but managed to stave off the Japanese long enough for Halsey to start moving from the north, where the bulk of our task force lay. In the meantime, a terrific battle took place. We could hear it but could not see it.

We are now carrying survivors to a replacement port. We are underway and trying to do all in our power to make these unfortunates comfortable. They are all ambulatory cases on our ship, and we are spared the unpleasant ceremonies which take place at sundown on the other ships in our convoy, most of which are carrying seriously wounded. All the ships lower their flags to half-mast—and the dead are turned over to Davy Jones.

Most of the men we have are suffering from exposure (50 hours in the water), saltwater sores, sunburn, shock, colds, and general exhaustion. So we baby them—feed them broth and steak, clothe them with all our spare equipment, and in general try to make them feel as happy as is possible under the circumstances. Many of them won't realize for weeks what happened and will probably suffer nervous reactions. Their descriptions of the waterless hours on overloaded rafts are chilling. Many of them died on the rafts, and all of them were in constant terror of the sharks that followed them. We have nineteen officer-survivors, and the appreciation they evidence is surely gratifying.

Speaking of sharks, one of the men just escaped from a shark. The beast took the seat of his trousers and left five deep tooth scratches in his stern.

We should arrive in this new port by the 4th, and from there I don't know just what we'll be doing. At any rate, everything is going well, and we have plenty of food and ammunition.

I have a new station at general quarters. I am in charge of the forward battery in addition to my recognition duties. In lulls between attacks we have lots of fun, lying around on mattresses and life jackets and telling tall stories. Then the cooks come around with iced tea, coffee, sandwiches—and at night with cake and hot chocolate or whatever seems appropriate.

After the third day the natives began coming out after clothes and food and medical attention. I'm enclosing a photograph of a typical outrigger load. Most of them speak English and know how to bargain. Their end of the bargain is usually confined to the money the Japanese issued them. It is worth 50 percent of ours, according to them.

I want you to know that I'm very healthy and happy and that I love you. Say hello to all, and don't let long pauses in correspondence concern you.

LST 169 beached at Leyte,
October 1944

Natives approach ship to barter
at Leyte, October 1944

8 November '44

It's been so long since I've written I think I'd better say hello, although I'm about as tired as I'm ever able to get in this life. I was busy all day running around Hollandia Harbor and town and back in the hills of New Guinea trying to get supplies to solve the eternal problem of eating. But now I've drunk so much coffee that I'm not sleepy. We haven't had any mail since we left the Admiralty Islands a month ago, and since we are going about, I suppose it won't catch up with us for at least another month.

It seems that the British are very careful to have at least one ship present at every invasion and at every port, so when it's all over they'll be able to say they were "in on it," and put in their claims. There are several scrupulously clean Dutch ships here. They have *himmelblau* [sky blue] masts and red-cheeked sailors. The officers wear great campaign hats when ashore and use tidy little Javanese as orderlies. The natives here are somewhat in the background—as who wouldn't be when thousands of vehicles and men come swarming all over the place? New Guinea is a rich island. It must be or the wise Dutch wouldn't be bothering with it. Copra and palm oil are the big products. The palm trees are taller and more luxurious than at any place I've been.

The WACs have recently descended on this once monastic community of soldiers. I must admit that a woman is a sight not to be dismissed lightly, and, of course, everybody stares. They go about in a coverall uniform and return the hails and shouts of the men with, at worst, coy indifference.

We are leaving here shortly for another hauling job: men and materiel—where, I can't tell you at this time. But I do wish they'd get their supply line straightened out. The survivors we brought from the naval battle off Leyte about ate us out of provisions, and things are rather scarce. However, if I do say it myself, I have managed our commissary rather well, and we are frankly the envy of every ship in the harbor. Everybody is eating Spam and dehydrated things, and we are still making out with steaks, fresh apples and pears, and big Idaho potatoes. How long this will last I don't know, but in the meantime I wield the big whip in the galley and have reduced waste to the minimum, promoted soup, and sorted good from bad to preserve the fresh things religiously.

I'd like to get back to Leyte. I ordered a bolo knife from an ex-Philippino scout named Marciale Javies, who moseyed out to our ship one day in his outrigger canoe, and maybe I'll see him again. He has also promised bananas and coconuts and fresh corn. In spite of all the warnings, I intend to eat the corn because I like corn on the cob more than I fear ague or whatever one is supposed to get.

The survivors we had were a grateful and appreciative lot. Their descriptions of the tragic results of their particular engagement are rather grim: with three-fourths of the crew strewn about the deck, they abandoned ship, and sharks pestered them for fifty waterless hours. One of the destroyer survivors was a chap named Stallings, from Pittsburgh. His feet were badly sunburned, and the saltwater sores nearly drove him mad. But he is lucky compared to most of his shipmates. We gave them clothes and books to read and filled them with good food and beer. I think they really hated to leave us. We are so used to having lots of people aboard that the ship seems empty when we have only our ship's company.

I suppose today is Election Day and that Roosevelt has been re-elected. The Philippine invasion was staged just in time. MacArthur stepped on the beach, fulfilling his promise, and everything is perfectly lovely until you look at the chart and see how much we don't have. Not that political considerations bother me, but one cannot help noticing the obvious.

By the way, how is Mrs. Roosevelt doing? Has she had any more teas for the Young Communist League or initiated any more projects for the underprivileged? I can't keep in touch with the affairs of state, so I rarely ever think of them. I'm reading a good book now: *Young Man from Caracas*. If you haven't done so, read it. Lately I finished *The Late George Apley* and could hardly put it down. I enjoy his observations of the Irish of Boston. My other literary life is confined to *Bureau of Supply and Accounts Manual, Navy Cook Book* and *Watch Officer's Guide*. Chapters like "Disbursing Officers' Vouchers," "Differences in Piping One-star, Two-star and Three-star Admirals," and "How to make Chicken a la King with Veal and No Mushrooms," are vital and stimulating, but I'd rather take a little 190 and fruit juice any day—or night.

Say hello to all our mutual acquaintances.

Tacloban

The peaceful plop of paddles
Which guide a rigged canoe,
Are heard about the fantail
Where gathered is the crew.

When sun is set the sailors sit
On capstan, box, or bitt,
And talk and smoke,
Talk and smoke,
Chew the fat,
Bat the breeze,
Or hug the rail and spit.

The friendly Philippino boys
Are waving to them now;
They've come to sell their bolo knives
For shirts, or soap, or chow.

Jules
8 November '44

10 November '44

Today we beached on one of the loveliest of all islands of the Southwest Pacific. I say this without the necessary authority of having seen them all in order to speak so, but I am reasonably sure that few others could offer more.

Nuemfor Island is a Dutch possession of the Schonten group, not far off the northwest coast of New Guinea. It is about thirty miles in length and conspicuous for its tall trees. It is volcanic, like so many of them, and supports a luxurious vegetation that is practically impenetrable. I know because Behinken and Mike, the two good storekeepers who make life so pleasant for me, and I stumbled through the thick undergrowth for hours without really getting anywhere. In the course of our travels, which were promoted primarily by a desire to procure some fresh fruits and vegetables if possible, we gathered shells, ate papaya, whacked off the ends of coconuts and drank the milk, went swimming when we were in the mood, tried to catch brilliant parrots that flew shrieking from our range, found the smelly remains of a dead Japanese soldier, ate small green grapefruits, visited native villages built over the water, bargained with them for their wood carvings, and gave cigarettes to five-year-old boys.

An army private who was tired of hauling coral fill was easily persuaded to take us to some remote native village on the other side of the island. While the road made a Kentucky trail look like a highway, it was indeed worth it. At an early stage in the campaign, a grizzled ancient, garbed in at least three square inches of loin cloth, emerged from the bush with a friendly greeting and promptly ensconced himself on the fender of the truck and directed us to proceed. He wore paper clips as earrings and a piece of Pabst beer can for a bracelet. He is either the actual leader of the natives he brought us to, or their self-appointed guide and director of traffic and convention chairman wrapped in one.

About fifty natives clustered about us at the first stop. "Americans good, Japanese no good," they would say, over and over again. They all seemed so friendly, except some dowagers who maintained both their reserve and their dignity by refusing to get up, possibly in fear of disturbing their amazing hair-dos. Little girls were with child either à la papoose or in utero, and offspring of all sizes scampered all over the place. Gradually they brought out their wood carvings. Mike obtained a truly artistic image, which shows an excellent feeling for design, proportion and color, by giving them his shirt. I asked one old man, who seemed to have some authority, to get us ten papayas and ten coconuts. He uttered some orders, and up the tall trees of the grove in which this village was located scampered happy little boys. I gave him a cellophane-wrapped White Owl, which he promptly smoked, cellophane and all.

At one point in the ten-mile trip, we had as many as thirty dusky, squirming natives bouncing around the truck. One old campaigner had a Jap rifle, which he fired periodically every so often to the high glee of the crowd. Nothing pleases them so much as bits of cloth or a hat. The spectre of dozens of small boys running around with hats and nothing else but the atmosphere creates a rather top-heavy effect. The older people are clothed rather to fit their moods. One man wore three shirts—one on top of the other while the majority wore nothing but a cloth postage stamp. Some of the women wrap loin cloths about them; many of them are content with a few strands of palm. In any case, they all seem happy, and one can only reflect how untouched they are by the complexities of civilization and modern conveniences. They require absolutely nothing which nature does not provide them in abundance. Some of them have skin diseases, but most of them seem healthy and clean. They swim a lot and probably have healthy digestive organisms if coconut milk affects them the way it does me.

We are taking some more army engineers from here to Leyte. We're supposed to leave tomorrow, but I seriously doubt if we'll get off the beach without some aid—we ran so far up on it. Personally I wouldn't mind spending a few weeks here in the restful atmosphere of surf and sand, outrigger canoes, cheerful natives and an abundant nature. We haven't received any mail for five weeks now. We chase about, and it chases us. Soon it will be Thanksgiving and then Christmas, and it will be hard to imagine in this soft, warm climate.

Good night.

27 November '44

It certainly was good to receive your letters and hear the news since we hadn't had any mail for nearly seven weeks, and that's a rather long time on a ship that has no recreational facilities.

Speaking of recreational features, the natives provide that in a big way. They came out in their outriggers the other day with four game-cocks, and all of them were snapped up in the trading. So for a week we had cockfights on the tank deck and the incongruous sounds of boastful crowing aboard ship. Then one day a native came with a monkey. The woman who had him wanted some rice and wheat flour, so being keeper of those keys, I got the monkey. The skipper heard about it and forbade the presence of a monkey on board. I disobediently arranged to have the deal consummated at the starboard bow while someone engaged the skipper's attention on the port quarter. In that manner my agents and I had the secret pleasure of the monkey's company for three days. He was a clever little thing—beautiful coat—just three months old. It would imitate our actions in a most engaging manner, and soon we of the inner circle had the pleasure of going about with a monkey on one shoulder and a highly colored gamecock on the other. But the other day somebody was awakened too early by the lusty crowing, and the skipper ordered all pets off except Kodiak. This, I think, is a great mistake because pets are terrific morale boosters, but I am thankful that I, at least, have learned the cardinal principle of military life some years ago, which, as you know, is obedience, even though somewhat tardily invoked in this case.

We have been subjected to some exciting air attacks lately and seem to spend most of our time at battle stations. The other day we had a perfect view of the kind of thing you read about but hardly ever expect to see. A Jap "Hamp" (small fighter-bomber) came buzzing in. A small ship astern of us (we were anchored at the time) opened fire; so did we, and with telling effect: when he realized he was hit, the Japanese crashdived into an ARD (floating dry dock), which carried a damaged destroyer in its ways at the time, thus hitting two ships at once. This took place less than four hundred yards off our beam in the middle of the day (noon exactly), affording us a perfect, uninterrupted view. An explosion followed, and it looked like the end for both ships. But they put out the fire and found that the damage wasn't as great as it appeared it would be. Only one man was killed. He was in his sack, where no one should be at that hour. The pilot was dissolved.

Thanksgiving Dinner, 1944, Leyte, Philippine Islands
Left to right: Fern, Horton, Idencio, Mike, Behuken, Ell, Bierschmitt, Turton, Green, and Ries.

Less than fifteen minutes later another plane came over. We hit him, then he made like he was going to crashdive us (the Japs are doing a lot of that lately), and I must say that I was scared. He changed his mind, however, and strafed us, then crashed into the sea about a mile off. No one was hurt. This is the luckiest ship.

3 December '44

Since I last wrote we have had several more air attacks, but not so close and cozy. We had time for an uninterrupted Thanksgiving dinner. The turkeys we had saved for the occasion were really delicious. The photographer took pictures of the turkeys and the staffs of my departments. The dehydrated cranberries turned out all right too. We had the usual accessories and lots left over. In the afternoon a group of twenty Philippine guerillas came aboard with many speeches about "our liberators." These natives were armed to the teeth with bolo knives and pistols and were in search of clothes and food. Before we led them into the galley, they sang a Philippine song of liberation, directed by their "lieutenant," then wound up the sangerfest with a vocal tribute to "Gen er Ale Nu au Toor" to the tune of the Notre Dame Victory march. They had brought their girlfriends with them, so the visitation was very popular. Some of the Philippine girls are very pretty, and Idencio is having a field day. They ate most of what was left of the turkey, although they left convinced that it was a big chicken. "Turkey and Thanksgiving" just didn't seem to register in spite of Idencio's translations.

Yesterday I went into the capital of the particular island off which we are lying at present. About 30,000 people in a sea of mud. It is raining about one half the time now. All the heavy army traffic has made the dirt streets each into a lake, and each step is fraught with peril. After a visit to the post office, Chief Imman and I started out for some fun, and I promptly fell into a four-foot mud hole in the midst of the main thoroughfare. That was fun enough for him, he said, but we went on and spent three rainy, muddy but pleasant hours sightseeing, talking with guerillas, soldiers, sailors, drinking tuba (a beer made from coconut palm hearts), whiskey distilled from the same, and sake (which I hadn't tasted since Saipan), and eating delicious crabs, rice cakes and fried chicken.

Now that the holiday season is more or less here, I suppose Cincinnati is bristling with Christmas displays and holly. Maybe we'll get a little Philippine pine for a Christmas tree. With the palms we could have a nice crèche. If you don't hear from me beforehand, I hope you all have an excellent Christmas and lots of fun. Sometime we find it as difficult to get mail off as to receive it, so don't worry about long lapses. Merry Christmas.

18 December '44

We're on the move again. Now that we're departed, I can tell you that we had been in Leyte harbor again. We were there for the invasion and ten days, then to New Guinea, then back to Leyte. We've had some mechanical trouble, and now we're going somewhere for necessary reconditioning.

I was in Tacloban, the capitolio, the other day with Idencio, the steward. We had a wonderful time. We sloshed through a lot of mud, but it was worth it. Naturally the natives are tickled to see a Philippino in a U.S. uniform, and he really cuts a lot of ice with the women. When I go with him, we never worry about enough to eat or drink. We just get invited in, and there we are sitting down to a dinner of chicken, crab, kamote (sweet potato), guava, rice, and tuba, the local dago red which is made out of the sap in coconut fronds. The old man or the boyfriend is either helping the army unload ships or fighting with the guerillas, so everything is lovely.

These people are certainly casual about living and sanitary arrangements. Their attempts at cleaning up the house are at best feeble, and the toilet is little more than a hole in the floor. But the women manage to keep looking neat and clean, thanks to a seeming natural fondness for laundering and thanks to the Singer Sewing Machine Co., whose zealous evangelists have managed to place their machines in the most incongruous and unexpected places. Perhaps not, since they seem to get such satisfaction out of thwacking and slapping and scrubbing their clothes till they're paper-thin but clean. I think all that pummelling is good for their dispositions as boxing is for confined men. I noticed some of the women taking a fiendish delight in knocking the hell out of their husbands' shirts.

I hope you have a good Christmas.

23 December '44

Now comes the holiday season once more, and for me, the first afloat. It will probably be late in the month, perhaps on New Year's Eve, when we arrive at our next destination. I suppose all the mail that began coming our direction when we were off Tacloban, Leyte, will gang up there, and we'll probably receive it sometime in April.

I suppose Christmas will be right gay aboard the *169*. We'll have turkey and all that, including plum pudding and hard sauce. I doubt if we'll have the brandy for the pudding because the skipper is pretty squeamish about letting it out. The sick bay carries about six quarts, but since they didn't even get it out for the survivors we carried, I can't hope to persuade him to let it go for the pudding. He knows it would never get as far as the pudding anyway.

But the Christmas tree which the carpenter's mate made is already installed, lights and all, and the records of Holy Night, Adeste Fidelis, Messiah, Star of Bethlehem, etc. are blaring right now all over the ship. The skipper, who claims he is an atheist (he hasn't been in a foxhole) and a music lover, is deeply shocked and upset.

Idencio, the steward, has developed an intense interest in the welfare of my mother. He asks about you all the time, and if you mention anything about him in a letter, I tell him, and he flutters about like a pigeon. Today I told him he would be welcome at our home at any time, and in five minutes he produced a tenderloin such as you've never dreamed of—garlic salt and a kind of fish sauce purchased in Tacloban. He is really a fine person.

25 December '44

Well, we have had quite a nice Christmas. The little tree the carpenter made is quite a success, and the lights twinkle on it merrily. On Christmas Eve the skipper conducted a service on the main deck just as the sun set, and the star of Bethlehem began to shine. After that there was beer (big favor), and at 11 PM this old commissary officer broke down with cheese sandwiches, cinnamon cake and coffee. Those who bothered to get up next day had fresh eggs, fresh apples and fried canned ham (this latter is an excellent item by the way). At one o'clock we had turkey, dressing, mashed dehydrated sweet potatoes, dehydrated cranberries, succotash, pineapple upside-down cake, ice cream, fruit cordial. At supper we had tuna salad (everybody likes tuna), turkey soup, plum pudding. At ten o'clock we had sweet rolls and hot chocolate. So if anybody went hungry, it wasn't my fault.

I hope you all had a nice Christmas.

30 December '44

Well, here we are in port. May be here for some weeks getting an overhaul. This is a good harbor, and there's a rather complete base here. It's the same place to which we brought the survivors some weeks ago. It is more attractive scenically than Leyte and not quite as rainy. The natives here keep well to the hills, but they come around occasionally with bananas and colorful fishing spears, which are just a bit too long for souvenir value. When we're in port, my work begins. But I always manage to include a few by-trips on my jaunts to the supply depot. Also there is a very snappy little officer's club on the beach—surrounded by luxurious vegetation and overlooking the blue waters of the harbor. Here one can drink whiskey, brandy, and Iron City beer at nominal fees. Also one can get an occasional glimpse of a female—a WAC or Red Cross girl, usually escorted by some ranking officer. I understand that one can get a date with a WAC provided he secures a jeep, carries sidearms and avoids looking evil in the eyes of the MPs. That sounds a little like too much bother, but then maybe it's worth the bother to the men who have been out here so long—many of them over thirty months.

I suppose I've seen more movies since I've been out in the Pacific than I have in the past ten years. I seldom go off the ship to see one, but when we are tied up alongside a ship that has one and I can see the screen from our ship in a comfortable position—well there I am. Tonight as I sat on the conning bridge, I could see six of them going on around us. But I concentrated on the screen set up on the bow of a destroyer alongside. Double feature, cigar, full moon, cool breezes.

The first one was a strange one about dreams and the supernatural called *Flesh and Fantasy*. Musical background by Alexandre Tansman.

U.S.S. LEYTE (ARG-8)

THE DAILY NEWS

9 JANUARY 1945

WASHINGTON:

CONTINUING SNOW BLANKETED NORTH CENTRAL STATES AND IS EXPECTED TO REACH EIGHT INCHES IN NORTH ILLINOIS. SNOW FELL IN INDIANA AND SOUTH MICHIGAN. SNOW OR FREEZING RAIN WAS FORECASTED FOR MANY EASTERN STATES AND RAIN FOR SOUTH CENTRAL STATES. BITTER COLD GRIPPED THE NORTH LAKES REGION WITH A LOW OF TWENTY-NINE BELOW AT LANDOLAKES WISCONSIN. POTHDAM IN UPPER NEW YORK HAD AN UNOFFICIAL LOW OF FORTY-EIGHT BELOW. THE NATIONS HIGHEST WAS SEVENTY-SEVEN AT BROWNSVILLE TEXAS. THE ARMY SENT SOLDIERS TO ERIE PENNSYLVANIA WITH TRUCKS, BULLDOZERS AND SNOWPLOWS TO HELP CLEAR ROADS SO WAR MUNITIONS COULD MOVE. FREIGHT CARS WERE TIED UP IN THE YARDS. THREE HUNDRED SOLDIERS CAME WITH MORE ON THE WAY. IN BUFFALO, WHERE WEEKS SNOW TOTALLED OVER NINETEEN INCHES PLEADED FOR MEN TO CLEAR SNOW HOLDING UP WAR SHIPMENTS BUT GOT ONLY ONE HUNDRED THIRTY EIGHT CIVILIANS. THE ARMY SENT SOLDIERS IN AND TWO HUNDRED SAILORS WERE ALREADY WORKING. IT IS SAID THAT FIVE THOUSAND FREIGHT YARDS WERE TIED UP AND WAR PLANTS ARE GETTING SHORT OF COAL. ONE HUNDRED TWENTY JAPANESE-AMERICAN SOLDIERS FROM FORT SNELLING ARE DELIVERING COAL TO FUEL-SHORT HOMES IN MINNEAPOLIS AND ST. PAUL. THEY WERE CHOSEN FROM FIVE HUNDRED SOLDIER VOLUNTEERS.

NEW YORK:

FILM DAILY, POLL OF FILM CRITICS OVER THE NATION VOTED THE BEST STARRING PERFORMANCES OF LAST YEAR WERE BING CROSBY IN "GOING MY WAY" AND JENNIFER JONES IN "SONG OF BERNADETTE". OTHER BEST MALE STAR PERFORMANCES WERE SPENCER TRACY IN "A GUY NAMED JOE" GARY COOPER IN "THE STORY OF DOCTOR WASSELL", AND FREDERIC MARCH IN "ADVENTURES OF MARK TWAIN". OTHER BEST FEMININE STARS WERE INGRID BERGMAN IN "GASLIGHT", GREER GARSON IN "MADAME CURIE", AND BETTE DAVIS IN "MR. SKEFFINGTON".

LIMA OHIO:

A FIRE WHICH STARTED IN THE MILNER HOTEL ALSO THREATENED SIX BUSINESS HOUSES. A WOMAN DIED AFTER LEAPING FROM THE HOTEL'S THIRD FLOOR.

NEW HAMPSHIRE LEADS NATION:

NEW HAMPSHIRE LED THE NATION IN THE SIXTH WAR LOAN WITH TWO HUNDRED TWENTY ONE PERCENT OF ITS QUOTA. IT RECEIVED THE TREASURY'S COMPLIMENTS FOR SUCH AN OUTSTANDING ACCOMPLISHMENT. MILWAUKEE WON THE BOND CONTEST AMONG EIGHT CITIES. THE STANDINGS OF THE RUNNERUPS WERE PITTSBURGH, PHILADELPHIA, WASHINGTON DC, LOSANGELES, BOSTON, ST. LOUIS, AND LAST, SANFRANCISCO.

HONOLULU:

PITTSBURGH'S EDGAR JONES THREW TWO TOUCHDOWN PASSES AS NAVY BEAT THE ARMY AIRFORCE FOURTEEN TO NOTHING IN A GAME DECIDING THE PACIFIC OCEAN AREAS SERVICE FOOTBALL CHAMPIONSHIP.

WASHINGTON:

CAMERA FANS, MOVIES, AND PHOTOGRAPHERS WILL GET MUCH SMALLER FILM SUPPLIES THIS YEAR. MOVIES MAY HAVE TO POSTPONE THIRTY BIG FILMS. CAMERA FILM FOR CIVILIANS WILL BE THE LOWEST YET. WPB SAID GREATER MILITARY NEED IS THE REASON.

WASHINGTON:

SENATOR JOHNSON, COLORADO DEMOCRAT, URGES ONE HUNDRED THOUSAND YOUNG MEN BE STARTED IN FLYING TRAINING EACH YEAR, SCHOOLING TO CONTINUE FOR FOUR OR FIVE YEARS WITH STUDY IN AIR ENGINEERING. HE SAYS "THIS WOULD GIVE US TRAINED RESERVE OF FIRST CLASS FLYING MEN AND BE THE GREATEST SINGLE THING WE COULD DO FOR NATIONAL PREPAREDNESS". HE SAID WE USED TO TAKE FOUR YEARS TO TRAIN BOMBER PILOTS AND "NOW WE TRY TO DO IT IN FIVE MONTHS".

Excerpts from 9 January 1945, U.S.S. *Leyte, The Daily News*

(PAGE TWO)

MILWAUKEE:
THE FIRST WISCONSIN NATIONAL BANK WAS CREDITED WITH AN ASSIST WHEN A SOLDIER IN FRANCE POPPED THE 'QUESTION TO HIS BEST GIRL. PVT. ROBERT GUENTHER OF SHEBOYGAN WAS THINKING OF BUYING A RING FOR CATHERINE GENSKI OF MILWAUKEE WHEN ORDERED OVERSEAS. HEHAS AN ACCOUNT IN THE BANK AND WROTE LAST MONTH ASKING WOULD THE BANK PLEASE BUY A DIAMOND RING AND PRESENT IT TO HER FOR HIM. SATURDAY SHE WAS INVITED TO THE BANK. CASHIER A.G. CASPER READ PART OF THE LETTER THEN BLUSHING GAVE HER A PACKAGE TIED WITH WHITE SILK RIBBON. OUT CAME A CORSAGE AND THEN THE RING. MISS GENSKI SAID "OH". THAT WAS THAT AS FAR AS THE BANK WAS CONCERNED. PVT. GUENTHER CAN TAKE IT FROM THERE.

LOS ANGELES:
FOG HALTED THE THIRD ROUND OF THE 72 HOLE LOSANGELES OPEN GOLF TOURNEY TODAY WITH MANY OF THE STARS AMONG THE LATE PLAYERS UNABLE TO FINISH BECAUSE THEY COULDN'T SEE THE COURSE. AMONG THOSE WHO DID FINISH BEFORE THE FOG CLOSED IN WERE BYRON NELSON, TOLEDO OHIO, AND SGT. E.J. HARRISON, WRIGHT FIELD, DAYTON OHIO WHO SHARED THE LEAD WITH 213. NELSON HAD A 70 AND SGT. HARRISON A 69 FOR THE DAY. PAR FOR THE COURSE IS 71. THE PLAYERS STYMIED BY THE FOG TODAY WILL ATTEMPT TO FINISH THEIR ROUNDS TOMORROW BEFORE TH FINAL 18 HOLES PLAY BEGINS.

BASKETBALL SCORES:
CHAMPAIGN ILL., UNIVERSITY OF MICHIGAN 43 --- UNIVERSITY OF ILLINOIS 38 SATURDAY NIGHT. IOWA CITY, IOWA, IOWA 41 --- MINNESOTA 34. GREATLAKES, GREATLAKES BLUEJACKETS 59 --- NOTRE DAME 38.

ICE HOCKEY:
BUFFALO BISONS THREE --- PITTSBURGH HORNETS TWO.

WASHINGTON:
MORE THAN THIRTY THOUSAND OF THE SEVEN HUNDRED THOUSAND ENLISTED NEGRO SOLDIERS IN THE ARMY INTEND TO RETURN TO FULLTIME SCHOOLING AFTER THE WAR. THE WAR DEPARTMENT, REPORTING A SURVEY, ALSO SAID SEVEN PERCENT OF ALL NEGRO TROOPS HAVE DEFINITE PLANS TO START A BUSINESS OF THEIR OWN AFTER THE WAR WHILE FOUR PERCENT INTEND TO OPERATE FARMS.

WASHINGTON:
SENATE REPUBLICANS ARE CHARGING ANEW THAT PRESIDENT ROOSEVELT HAS FAILED TO PROVIDE LEADERSHIP IN FOREIGN AFFAIRS. COMMENTING ON THE PRESIDENT'S MESSAGE TO CONGRESS, SENATOR TAFT OF OHIO, CHAIRMAN OF THE SENATE REPUBLICAN STEERING COMMITTEE, TOOK THE LEAD IN CRITICIZING THE PRESIDENTS ADDRESS. HE SAID THE ADDRESS CONTAINED NO EVIDENCETHAT THE ADMINISTRATIONS WAVERING AND SECRETIVE FOREIGN POLICY WAS TO BE CHANGED. MEANWHILE SENATOR PEPPER, FLORDIA DEMOCRAT, ALWAYS A CONSISTENT ADMINISTRATION SUPPORTER SAID "THE PRESIDENT HAS CHALLENGED ALL OF US TO PUT FORTH OUR BEST EFFORTS IN MAKING THE PEACE".

WASHINGTON:
THE POSSIBILITY OF THE UNITED STATES JOINING IN INTERNATIONAL MACHINERY TO GOVERN STRIFE TORN LIBERATED AREAS OF EUROPE UNTIL THEIR OWN PEOPLES CAN TAKE OVER PEACEABLY IS RECEIVING SERIOUS ATTENTION IN WASHINGTON. IT MAY OFFER A PLAN IN THE VIEW OF SOME OFFICIALS BY WHICH PRESIDENT ROOSEVELT CAN MAKE THE UNITED STATES POWER AND INFLUENCE WORK FOR THE PRINCIPLES OF THE ATLANTIC CHARTER. IT IS EMPHASIZED HOWEVER WE WOULD BACK SUCH MEASURES UNTIL THE PEOPLE ACHIEVES ITS OWN STABILITY AS IN FRANCE. EXACTLY WHAT THE PRESIDENT WILL DO REMAINS TO BE WORKED OUT IN OR AFTER HIS MEETING WITH CHURCHILL AND STALIN.

ATHENS:
THE BRITISH FOUGHT WITH REARGUARDS PROTECTING WITHDRAWAL OF LEFTWING ELAS FORCES INTO THE HILSS A FEW MILES WEST AND NORTHWEST OF ATHENS.

UNDATED EUROPEAN WAR:

THE U.S. FIRST ARMY ON THE WESTERN FRONT SEIZED CONTROL OF ONE OF TWO MAIN GERMAN SUPPLY ROUTES IN BELGIUM BULGE IN GAINS UP TO THREE MILES ON A THIRTY MILE NORTHERN FLANK OF GERMAN PENETRATION. MEANWHILE A ONE MILE GAIN BY THE THIRD ARMY TIGHTENED THE SQUEEZE FROM THE SOUTH. GERMANS COUNTERED WITH SIX OR MORE ATTACKS ALONG THE FRONT INCLUDING PUSHES BOTH IN FAR NORTH AND FAR SOUTH. MAJOR SUPPLY ROUTES WERE CUT BY AMERICANS A FEW MILES NORTHEAST OF LAROCHE AT A SPOT EIGHT MILES NORTH OF HOUFFALIZE AND ALSO WEST OF THERE AND IN A THIRD PLACE IN THE SAME GENERAL AREA. A FRONT DISPATCH SAID FIRST ARMY GAINS PUT IT ON HEIGHTS WHERE IT CAN LOOK DOWNHILL ON GERMANS IN THE BULGE. AMERICANS ALSO ARE MENACING VON RUNDSTEDTS NORTH-SOUTH HIGHWAY INTO HIS BASE AT HOUFFALIZE IN THE CENTER OF THE BULGE. THEY ARE CLOSING IN ON LAROCHE ON THE WEST AND BREAKING ACROSS AMBLEVE RIVER INTO GERMAN STRONG POSTIONS FIVE TO TEN MILES SOUTH AND SOUTHWEST OF STAVELOT. THEY GAINED UP TO THREE MILES SOUTHWEST OF STAVELOT. THE CAPTURE OF LAROCHE WOULD THREATEN GERMAN FORCES RESISTING BRITISH SECOND ARMY PRESSURE AT THE WEST END OF THE BULGE IN ROCHE- FORT AREA. THE BRITISH GAINED A MILE SOUTHEAST OF MARCHE, THE THIRD ARMY DRIVING NORTH GAINED A MILE ALONG THE THREE MILE FRONT THREE TO SIX MILES WEST OF BASTOGNE AND ON THE EAST ARE WITHIN A MILE AND A HALF OF WILTZ. GERMANS WERE REPORTED TO HAVE PLANTED SMALL BRIDGEHEAD ACROSS MASS RIVER FAR TO THE NORTH IN EAST HOLLAND, BUT MAJOR GERMAN ATTACKS WERE IN THE STRASBOURG AREA TOWARD THE SOUTH END OF THE LONG FRONT. THE GERMANS ATTACKED IN FOUR PLACES NORTH OF STRASBOURG. THEY HAVE A SIX MILE BRIDGEHEAD THREE MILES DEEP IN AN AREA EIGHT MILES NORTH OF STRASBOURG AND THIS WAS REINFORCED WITH AT LEAST FIVE TANKS FERRIED ACROSS THE RHINE. HERE THEY ARE SIX MILES FROM HAGUENAU. THEY ALSO ARE ATTACKING DRUSENHEIM, EIGHT MILES EAST OF HAGUENAU. THE GERMANS NORTH OF HERE ARE ATTACKING WITH TANKS IN AN AREA SOUTHEAST OF THE FRENCH-GERMAN BORDER TOWN OF WISSEMBOURG IN NORTHEAST FRANCE. THEN NINETEEN MILES BELOW STRASBOURG THE GERMANS BROUGHT FIFTEEN TANKS ACROSS THE RHINE AND RECAPTURED NEUNKIRCH. SNOW AND CLOUDS AGAIN DENIED THE ALLIES CLOSE AIR SUPPORT.

FOURTEEN HUNDRED U.S. HEAVIES WITH NEARLY SEVEN HUNDRED FIGHTERS POURED THREE THOUSAND TONS OF BOMBS ON FIVE FREIGHT YARDS, TWO RHINE BRIDGES AND SIX RAIL YARDS BETWEEN HAMM AND KARLSRUHE. THEY BOMBED BY INSTRUMENT IN FIFTY BELOW COLD. NINE BOMBERS AND ONE FIGHTER ARE MISSING. SATURDAY NIGHT ONE THOUSAND RAF HEAVIES HIT HANAU LOSING TEN PLANES AND SUNDAY NIGHT TWO FORCES OF RAF HEAVIES TOTALLING PROBABLY ONE THOUSAND PLANES HIT MUNCIH TWICE IN TWO HOURS.

FIELD MARSHAL SIR BERNARD MONTGOMERY WHO NOW COMMANDS FOUR ARMIES ABOVE THE GERMAN BULGE INCLUDING AMERICAN FIRST AND NINTH, PRAISED COURAGE AND FIGHTING QUALITY OF AMERICAN FIGHTING MEN AND SAID THEY WERE RESPONSIBLE FOR STOPPING THE GERMAN DRIVE INTO BELGIUM. HE SAID THE BATTLE IS FAR FROM OVER BUT THAT THE GERMANS "HAVE BEEN HALTED THEN SEALED OFF AND NOW WE ARE IN THE PROCESS OF WIPING THEM OFF". HE SAID THE TENACITY OF AMERICAN SOLDIERS REALLY SAVED THE SITUATION BY STANDS AT ST. VITH, BASTOGNE, AND SOUTH OF MONSCHAU. HE PRAISED ESPECIALLY THE AMERICAN SECOND AND SEVENTH ARMORED DIVISIONS, THE EIGHTY SECOND AND ONE HUNDRED FIRST AIRBORNE AND ONE HUNDRED SIXTH INFANTRY. HE ALSO PRAISED THE STAND SOUTH OF MONSCHAU WHICH WAS MADE BY THE FIRST, SECOND, NINETY-NINTH AND THIRTIETH INFANTRY DIVISIONS. HE SAID HE TAKES HIS HAT OFF TO THE AMERICAN TROOPS. HE SAID THE SECOND MAIN REASON FOR THE HALTING OF THE GERMANS WAS GREAT ALLIED TEAM- WORK. HE PRAISED GENERAL EISENHOWER'S LEADERSHIP. HE SAID "I USED TO THINK ROMMEL WAS GOOD BUT VON RUNDSTEDT COULD KNOCK HIM FOR SIX. WE GOT HIS PICTURE UP ON THE WALL OF MY ROOM ALONGSIDE ROMMELS". IN SPEAKING OF EISENHOWER, MONTGOMERY TOLD WAR CORRESPONDENTS "IT GRIEVES ME WHEN I SEE UNCOMPLIMENTARY ARTICLES ABOUT HIM IN THE BRITISH PRESS. HE BEARS A GREAT BURDEN AND NEEDS OUR FULLEST SUPPORT HE HAS A RIGHT TO EXPECT IT AND IT IS UP TO ALL OF US TO SEE THAT HE GETS IT. AND SO I ASK ALL OF YOU TO LEND A HAND AND STOP THAT SORT OF THING. LET US ALL RALLY AROUND THE CAPTAIN OF THE TEAM AND SO HELP WIN THE MATCH. (CONTINUED ON PAGE 4)

(PAGE FOUR)

EUROPEAN WAR UNDATED CONTINUED:

NO ONE OBJECTS TO HEALTHY CRITICISM. IT IS GOOD FOR US. BUT LET US HAVE DONE WITH DESTRUCTIVE CRITICISM THAT AIMS A BLOW AT ALLIED SOLIDARITY THAT TENDS TO BREAK UP OUR TEAM SPIRIT AND THEREFORE HELPS THE ENEMY".

MAJ. GEN. VANDENBERG, COMMANDING THE NINTH AIRFORCESAID HIS FIGHTERBOMBERS KNOCKED OUT SEVEN THOUSAND GERMAN TRUCKS AND ONE THOUSAND TANKS IN TWELVE DAYS OF BATTLE. THEY SHOT DOWN FIVE HUNDRED GERMAN PLANES AND DESTROYED THREE HUNDRED ONE ON THE GROUND. THEY ALSO KNOCKED OUT MANY BRIDGES. HE SAID THE GERMAN STRATEGY WAS TO CAPTURE HUGE STORES OF GASOLINE. OFFICIAL ANNOUNCEMENT LAST WEEK SAID THE ALLIES LOST A HALF MILLION GALLONS OF GAS, OIL AND LUBRICATIONS WHICH VANDENBERG SAID WAS ONLY ONE PERCENT OF STOCKS IN THE FORWARD ZONES.

V-2 FLYING BOMBS CONTINUED TO FALL IN SOUTH ENGLAND.

THUNDERBOLTS OF THE TWELFTH AIRFORCE IN ITALY SET THE FORMER ITALIAN LINER ROMA AFIRE IN GENOA HARBOR. THE ROMA HAS BEEN CONVERTED INTO A CARRIER AND WAS ALSO HIT LAST JUNE. THE RAIN BOGGED THE ITALIAN FRONT BUT CANADIANS CUT OFF TWO GERMAN COMPANIES AND AN ARTILLERY UNIT NORTHWEST OF RAVENNA AND KILLED OR CAPTURED MOST.

MOSCOW SAID GERMAN COUNTERATTACKS TWENTY MILES NORTHWEST OF BUDAPEST FORCED RUSSIANS FROM ESZTERGOM ON THE DANUBE. FARTHER NORTH THE RUSSIANS ESTABLISHED A BRIDGEHEAD OVER TWELVE MILES DEEP ACROSS THE HRON RIVER AND CONTINUED TO GAIN IN BUDAPEST.

UNDATED PACIFIC WAR:
CARRIER TASK FORCES OF THE THIRD FLEET STRUCK AIRCRAFT, SHIPPING AND INSTALLATINS IN AROUND LUZON IN THE PHILIPPINES SATURDAY SHORTLY AFTER IT FINISHED A SWEEP OF FORMOSA AND KYUKYU ISLANDS. ADMIRAL NIMITZ SAID EARLY REPORTS SHOWED TWENTY SEVEN JAP PLANES DESTROYED, EIGHT OF THESE IN THE AIR AND FOURTEEN WERE DAMAGED. DETAILS OF OTHER DAMAGE ARE NOT YET AVAILABLE. ANOTHER SURFACE FORCE IN THE NORTH PACIFIC BOMBARDED SUIBACHI ON PARAMUSHIRO IN THE JURILES ON THE SAME DAY. LIBERATORS HIT IWO FOR THE THIRTIETH DAY AND MARINE PLANES STRAFED SUPPLY DUMPS IN THE PALAUS.

GENERAL MACARTHUR ANNOUNCED GROUND FORCES ON MINDORO CAPTURED PALUAN ON THE NORTHWEST COAST DESTROYEING JAP SUPPLY DUMPS AND INSTALLATIONS. SIXTH ARMY FORCE LANDED SEVEN MILES DOWN THE COAST FROM THE TOWN MAKING THE CAPTURE BY LAND. FOUR ENEMY PLANES ATTACKED MINDORO SHIPPING AND WERE DOWNED. SIX HUNDRED NINETY SEVEN MORE JAPS HAVE BEEN KILLED AND ELEVEN CAPTURED IN TWO DAYS OF MOPPING UP ON LEYTE. STRONG FORCES OF HEAVY BOMBERS SATURDAY HIT CLARK, NICHOLS, AND NIELSON AIRFIELDS ON LUZON DOING HEAVY DAMAGE AND DESTROYING EIGHTEEN PARKED PLANES. THERE WAS NO INTERCEPTION. OTHER PLANES ALSO HIT LUBANG FIELD AND AIR PATROLS DOWNED A FLOATPLANE OFF THE WEST COAST. MITCHELLS BLASTED FOUR AIRFIELDS ON NEGROS AND ONE WAS LOST TO FLAK. A PT BOAT SANK A FREIGHTER, TWO LUGGERS AND FOURBARGES AROUND CEBU. MINDANAO FIELDS WERE HIT AND TWENTY TWO TONS OF BOMBS POURED ON REFINERY AND INSTALLATIONS AT POMELAN IN THE CELEBES. RABUAL AIRDROMES AND SUPPLY AREAS WERE HIT WITH TWENTY TONS OF BOMBS FRIDAY AND SATURDAY WHILE OTHER PLANES ATTACKED TARGETS THROUGHOUT THE SOUTHWEST PACIFIC AREA. THE MOP UP ON MOROTAI HAS KILLED FIVE HUNDRED FIFTY EIGHT MORE JAPS AND CAPTURED EIGHTY SIX WITH TWELVE FRIENDLY NATIONALS RECOVED.

The next was one that I believe you would find enjoyable—*Janie*. It's quite good except for the end, which was overdone and more or less spoiled things. But it's still a lot of fun. It's about the bobbysocks crowd for the most part—perhaps older than that—high school girls and the army. Plenty of laughs. Do see it. (Incidentally Robert Benchley is in both movies.)

Tomorrow we will have the opportunity to hear Mass. Lots of ships around here. Give my New Year's best to your friends, and here is all my best for 1945 for you. I love you. Good night.

24 January '45

The other day a refrigerator ship arrived from New York. So now we have five tons of fresh meat and vegetables (cabbage and potatoes and onions) in our "deep freeze." Tonight we had some lamb chops and kidneys, and at noon we had T-bone steaks.

Idencio, the Philippino, was transferred today, and I shall surely miss him. He was not only an excellent cook but a congenial soul who was good to have around. When he told me good-bye, he looked so sad—I think he really didn't want to go. About fifteen others were transferred, and after living with people for nine months and seeing them so often, one gets to know them rather well. But all these men had been aboard since May 1943 and hope to get back to the States for thirty days.

1 February '45

Two of our officers were just transferred to other duty, but they were replaced by two men who are really an addition to the congeniality we have always managed to maintain, and they would be an addition to any group. Judson Kirby is a jg from Los Angeles. He used to be vice president of a West Coast insurance firm. He is about 38, nice looking and always ready for a good time. Douglas Saunders, warrant boatswain, is a Hollywood script writer. He worked for Warner Brothers and some radio concern. The other night we had the movie *Captains Courageous*. It features a two-masted schooner. Saunders is quite a sailor, and he not only sailed that particular schooner in the picture, but was technical advisor for the film re: nautical matters, gear, and lingo. He is excellent company.

Idencio and Fern

Never a dull moment. He is currently divorced from his fourth wife, who was Jean Parker, the cinema actress. He says it was the most sensational divorce in which he has ever been involved—made *Time* and *Newsweek*. He is a good officer. He knows deck work and gets things done. But he surely knows how to have a good time too. And I am glad to join him.

Saunders knows some nurses on the Dutch hospital ship *Maetsuycker*, which is commonly referred to as the "meat sucker." It is anchored close by. So two nights ago five of us from the *169* took out seven nurses for the evening. What a time. We came alongside their ship in our LCVP—and down the Jacob's ladder came the girls. They were all pretty and very sociable and glad to get off their ship for a time. (These are American army nurses, functioning aboard a Dutch-owned-and-operated ship.) We all went to the officer's club, which is open from 4 PM to 7 PM and had a beery and whiskeyish time, to say the least. Saunders was everywhere, telling stories, dancing, drinking, and everybody—including the skipper, who disappeared for a few minutes and produced two more girls—had a good time.

When the club closed it was dark—the moon shining, the surf pounding so rhythmically. Our small boat called for us at the officer's landing, and all twenty of us (by that time) piled in and sang all the way back to our ship. (We are tied up to the *Leyte*, a repair ship with 800 men. They have a tailor shop, barber shop, small stores, canteen, doctor, dentist, chaplain, and repair facilities, and on the other side of us is another LST also here for repairs. All the officers of these three ships get along beautifully. We visit each other and go to the club together and have meals on each other's ships.) Well, the other LST, the *223*, was having a party that night. A 15-piece orchestra (army) was procured and they played on deck from 7 PM to 9 PM. I had arranged a buffet supper and everything was lovely. We had turkey à la king, slaw, anchovies on toast, biscuits, melted cheese, coffee and three cases of beer. We had tables on the boat deck, and some of us wandered up there and listened to the music and ate supper. Then at nine o'clock we had a movie on the main deck under the stars. After the movie we had more beer, and at twelve we took the Red Cross girls back to their ship.

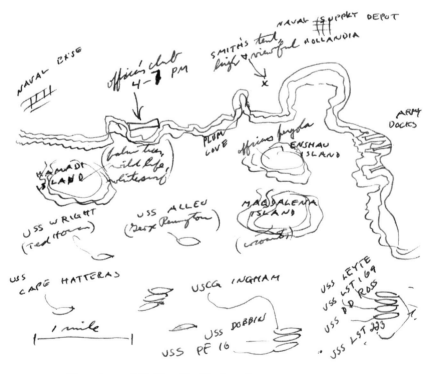

Drawing of Hollandia Harbor by Lieutenant Fern

One of the stewards at the officer's club is a skinny fellow named Wilson. He's our favorite. Yesterday we missed him, and it turns out he's in the hospital. He was trying to make a souvenir ashtray out of a Japanese hand grenade and pulled the pin out. It killed an onlooker and knocked a piece out of Wilson's head. We are taking up a collection to send him a box of cigars and possibly a bunch of flowers, which will have to be hibiscus mixed with nepa palm.

Last night we were to go dancing on the *223*, but it seems we never got around to it or to the movie. We had another buffet: ham, cheese, potato salad, slaw, olives, pickles, toast, coffee and beer. We played the Victrola, and everybody had a good time.

I guess if the U.S. public heard of such goings on, they wouldn't buy any war bonds, although it's not all a couch of hyacinths. Incidentally, I don't think the public gives enough credit to the women in the war. Some of the nurses have been overseas for 35 months without a leave. And they really work. The way casualties are pouring into the base hospital here, I know they work. There are three hospital ships in the harbor now. Soon they'll go back to the Philippines to bring down more. All the papers and movies are forever glorifying GI Joe. I think they better start recognizing women.

I suppose we will be here for some three or four more weeks. A lot of work is being done on the ship. Overhauled engines. Overhauling our two LCVPs (landing craft, vehicle, personnel), repairing the galley range, installing new plumbing, new railings, scraping the hull, painting the whole ship, installing a new gyro-compass system, new signal lights, etc., etc. I've been very busy and expected to supply everything. Quite a job. But as you must have gathered—when the golden hour comes, we recreate in no small way.

Greetings and love.

11 March '45

I don't know how much longer we'll be here, but I hope we get some excitement soon. We've missed two invasions on account of these engines. We're almost all fired now. The ship is entirely repaired, inside and out, and it looks as beautiful as an LST can look. The ugly duckling of the war, but a pretty useful one. We're not tied up to the *Leyte* anymore. She is gone. Monday I'll have a busy day—more supplies. This time machetes, knives and food.

A CG transport put in here the other day—fresh from the States. So I met the supply officer at the officer's club, and being a wino, he fell for my line and gave me five cases of fresh eggs, ten potatoes and one of onion—all rarities out here. The name of the ship is the *Admiral Capps.* New lot of ships—transports—of the General class and Admiral class are appearing from time to time. They are named for generals and admirals famed in American history.

I've been reading about rations, standing in lines, and more rationing. You all at home are undergoing more hardships than most of the servicemen, including myself. We have steak about twice a week, roast lamb and lamb chops once a week, pork chops once, liver once, veal once, roast beef once, creamed turkey, tuna salad, spaghetti and meatballs, sauerkraut and spare ribs. And we don't have to wait in line for things and don't have to worry about ration points and gas and liquor and all that. The powers that be have certainly organized this war very well. There are very few dissatisfied servicemen as far as I can see. And the Red Cross is doing a wonderful job of keeping people happy. The WACs are a help too. They are a leavening influence. The Russian merchant marines keep their wives aboard ship. If the war is to go on for long, I think that is a good idea. As it is, I don't see how it can do anything but go on and on if it takes such time for little Iwo Jima. Imagine what it will be when we get to Japan itself—and don't think the Japs are going to give up and compromise and all that tripe. Japanese airmen have been found (dead in their planes) shackled to their seats, i.e. "you don't come back," i.e. "you crash dive." That plus their will to die is a tough combination.

I forgot to tell you that I met two very interesting people the other night at the officer's club. I forget their names—army officers who have been released from the internment center at Cabanatuan near Manila. They were on their way home on the old Matoon liner *Monterey,* which put in here for a few days. They had been in that camp for three years, and among the things they observed, did, and experienced are the following:

1. They ate nothing but rice, an occasional mouse, and kamote (sweet potato).
2. They have gained 35 pounds each since their release less than 30 days ago.

3. They were told that the highest ranking army (U.S.) officer was lower than the lowest Japanese private, and hence there was no distinction as to rank, which is a violation of the international articles of war.

4. They had to work in the rice fields, and if they showed signs of shirking, they were beaten in the kidneys with rifle butts.

5. They said it was not uncommon to see 150 dead carried out in one day—dead from abuse and malnutrition.

6. Only the strongest survived.

7. These men were only beaten twice. They said that as long as you want to live, you might as well comply.

8. They had to make obeisance to the people who had them in charge, i.e. bowing, etc.

Guess we won't be here too long. So tonight might be our final fling. First it's the officer's club with a beautiful widow, then to a little island with a palm-hung beach—steaks, beer, and fruit juice—swimming in the starlight, lounging on the beach till midnight. Those lovely girls at home don't know what they're missing not being in the Red Cross—me for example!

Sea turtles are all around—going to the beach for hatching. Ain't nature grand? It's 75 days since the laying. Take care of yourself.

5 April '45

We arrived at this new port a few days ago, and now I have orders to report to the CG office at Leyte. So on my 32nd birthday I'll leave the *169* after almost a year of very interesting and stimulating duty.

Chapel Dedication
NAVAL BASE
NAVY 3205

The Naval Base Chapel, in all it's beauty, was accomplished by the untiring zeal and skill of Commodore James E. Boak, Commander Naval Base, Navy 3205, of Captain Dorrance K. Day, Chief of Staff, of the Architect and Engineers in charge, the construction organizations and volunteers.

May God reward their efforts.

SUNDAY
1 April 1945

Dedication

I   Glee Club: "A Perfect Toast"

II   Introduction: J. C. Durocher, Base Chaplain

III   Dedication Address:
>   Commodore James E. Boak,
>   Commander Naval Base

IV   Acceptance: M. H. Webb,
>   Lieut., ChC., USNR

V   Appreciation: C. H. Shulman,
>   Lieut., ChC., USNR

VI   Glee Club: The National Anthem

Program for Naval Base Chapel dedication

SUNDAY MASSES	CONFESSIONS	DAILY MASS
ABCD - 0700	Before each Mass.	Lady Chapel at
Base Chapel - 1130	After Evening Devotions.	Navy Base —
Base Chapel - 1700	Anytime by appointment	1145
	Base Chaplain's Office.	

```
*                              *
*         NOVENA               *
*   To The Miraculous Medal    *
*   TUESDAY 3 APRIL at 1830    *
*                              *
```

VICTORY DAY

1900 years ago, the world groaned under tyranny. Women and children, the old and weak, whole nations were bent under the yoke of slavery. THEN A DIVINE SOLDIER APPEARED who crushed the enemies of freedom and brought peace and victory to all His followers.

His battle wasn't an easy one: labor and fatigue, loneliness and discouragement, temptations and trials were His daily companions. But because He was more supernatural than natural, more of heaven than of earth, the Divine Soldier, Prince of Peace and King of Kings, won an all-out victory over His enemies, and brought peace on earth to men of good will. And the day He won that victory we still recall on Easter Sunday.

1900 years later Hitler and Hirohito are trying to crush people into slavery . . . and only Christ can stop them, only Christ can give the suffering world a true and lasting peace. Not only the Christ who fought on the plains of Galilee, on Calvary's mountain top . . but THE CHRIST WHO LIVES AND FIGHTS IN YOU! Without question, Christ the Divine soldier lives on in you!

STOP a minute. A Polish girl, her poor body frightfully abused by savage aryan soldiers, cries to you . . . BECAUSE YOU ARE OTHER CHRISTS.

LOOK. A little half-starved French baby raises its pitiful face to you, BECAUSE YOU ARE OTHER CHRISTS.

LISTEN. The millions of men rotting in prison camps lift their scourged and bleeding arms, and cry to you, BECAUSE YOU ARE OTHER CHRISTS.

Your fight is not an easy one. Like Christ, your Divine Captain, you taste the labor and fatigue of the long day; you feel the loneliness and discouragement of long nights spent far from loved ones. Trials and temptations are your daily companions, as they were Christ's.

But the sufferings of the Passion, the torments of His crucifixion were all made glorious on Easter Sunday, Victory Day, when Christ rose to victory glorious and immortal! He had conquered for all time the enemy of the human race.

And what a glorious career is yours, Soldier of Christ. Stay close to Him, and you will be sure of Victory. Offer your daily life with Christ in the Mass, and your whole day will take on the beauty, the splendor, the triumph of Christ. Receive often the Body of Christ in Communion . . and with St. Paul you will say every minute of your day: I live, now not I, but Christ — Christ, the Divine Soldier — lives in me!

And your Victory Day, the day when you liberate the world of suffering, will be another Easter Day . . the day when the world's greatest soldier stood forth victorious, resplendent, loved by the whole world whose freedom He had obtained!

OVER

MASSES THIS WEEK -

Sunday - April 1st - Mrs. Mary Monteleon (Dec.)
Monday - April 2nd - Charlotte Galczynski (Int.)
Tuesday - April 3rd - Shirley Flynn (Dec.)
Wednesday - April 4th - Dominic Ross (Dec.)
Thursday - April 5th - Lt. Gavin, USN., (Dec.)
Friday - April 6th - Frank Thering (Dec.)

AND DON'T FORGET - Next Friday, April 6th, is the First Friday of the Month - Mass - 1145 and Holy Hour - 1800 - 1900

****

May the grace of the Resurrected One be yours this Easter Day.

Your Chaplain,

Father Knott

U.S.S. PASTORES

11 April, 1945

DINNER MENU
****

Grapefruit Cocktail

Soup and Crackers

Celery and Olives

Grilled Sirloin Steaks

Fried Onions

Brown Gravy

Mashed Potatoes

Buttered Fresh English Peas

Bread and Butter

Cup Cakes - Ice Cream

Coffee

Dinner menu from neighboring ship

USA *Y-44*
23 April '45—30 October '45

The USA *Y-44* was a gasoline tanker owned by the United States Army, yet manned by the U.S. Coast Guard. These vessels were part of the Army Transportation Corps program that began 3 March 1944. But on 17 August 1944, recognizing that the Coast Guard could provide crews and training in relatively short periods of time, the army turned the operations of these tankers over to them.

Most of these 288 army craft served in the Southwest Pacific during the latter part of the war, but few of them had a home station. The tankers were relatively small (the *Y-44* on which Lieutenant Fern served was 162 feet long) and had shallow drafts to facilitate maneuvering among the islands and areas with various obstructions. When loaded, the tankers sat low in the water with their decks often awash, prompting some of their crew to refer to them as submarines.

As with all of Lieutenant Fern's assignments, he embraced his mission aboard the *Y-44*, which lasted approximately six months, until the Coast Guard crew was removed in October 1945.

27 April '45

Well, I'm all settled on the *Y-44*, a gasoline tanker. Good officers, twenty men, good food, a nice bunk and a desk in my room. I have a roommate, but he is a nice fellow. One of the officers was in my platoon at New London. There are only four of us. The captain is an old-timer—been all over the world and really knows his stuff. He is also a good timer, but too wise to get in trouble, and he and I have been having a really gay time since I came aboard in this Philippine port. I reported on 23 April—a year to the day I reported on the LST.

I left the LST early in the morning of my birthday and went to the receiving barracks. Then I went to the officer's club and sat quite alone, looking out to sea where the LST once was anchored. I felt like I had lost my home and was just beginning to feel sorry for myself when a Lieutenant Boyden came along. He was once a passenger with us. So we had a few drinks, then we had a delicious dinner at his mess, which is very nice. He also has a private club that is open rather late, and we were there having a good time. The bartender used to work at a Vine Street gin mill, and we had a delightful time. I stayed in his tent that night.

I met a bunch of happy souls at the receiving ship (barracks on the beach) and later came up to the Philippines with twelve of them. We came on the *Pastores*, a United Front liner, and it was just one big party cruise for eight days. What a time—just like our West Indies cruises. Same type of ship as the *Coamo* and others, only a bit older. This one was a transport in the last war and now is a refrigerator ship. Lettuce, celery, strawberries, steak, turkey, ice cream—and unofficially, brandy every night in someone's stateroom.

I meet more people out here from New London. It's amazing how small the world is. Sometimes I think the comparatively small Coast Guard is like a ladies' sewing club. Such gossip and "Do you know?" "He did?! Etc., etc." The club here has all of them beat. It is on a beautiful beach under a grove of palms and has several native-built nepa palm huts with open sides, bamboo benches, and here the natives in white run around with cold beer from Pittsburgh. Today I took a long swim, lay on the beach, listened to a band concert in a nearby enlisted men's recreation area—then went up to the huts and drank beer and listened to the latest gossip. What characters. Met two officers from Essington and two more classmates. I have the most fun with the old career men. They are full of the wildest stories, have no worries, see their wives once in a coon's age and seem to thrive on infinite quantities of alcohol in all forms without batting an eye. Some of the old surfmen can tell some thrilling stories of rescue at sea.

2 May '45

Yesterday, May 1, being International Labor Day, called for town meetings and labor gatherings. In front of the town hall in our homeport were erected several signs and a speaker's stand: "Long Live General MacArthur"; "Long Live Admiral Nimitz"; "Long Live President Osmena"; "Long Live the American Liberator"; "Long Live the Visayan Workers Association." Lots of the natives are employed by the army and navy. Many of the ships in the harbor are swarmed with Philippino boys who do the laundry and other details. At the officer's club the waiters are natives and run around like mad.

Several days ago I bought a gamecock named Mr. Calbayog. We keep him on the ship and take him to the beach every day so he can scratch in the gravel and eat bugs. We have a sandbox for him and feed him rice, bread, cabbage and anything left over. Every morning at daybreak he crows about six times and then subsides into a torpor similar to that in which the natives seem to engage.

Across the straits in Samar live many Philippino sailors and traders. They have rather elaborate sailboats, and they cart all manner of things to Tacloban to the market. They don't know the value of money and much prefer clothing and odds and ends to cash.

Calbayog perches on rail of the *LST 169* (Lieutenant Fern in middle)

10 May '45

We are finally underway with a load of aviation gasoline for some more northerly port. We had to go through the straits between Samar and Leyte and the trip was lovely. The waters are dotted with outriggers and sailboats loaded with natives on their way to markets farther down. Before we left Tacloban, we were loading gas near the airstrip. About a hundred yards astern of us a big transport was about to land, but since its motors were out, it couldn't make it and it crashed into the sea. We managed to save 26 people, but six drowned before the plane sank. I guess we'll get back to Tacloban sooner or later.

About 2:30 of the morning we sailed, Lieutenant Sweeney, a bibulous Irishman from another tanker, came over and stole Calbayog, my gamecock. I think he was hungry. If he killed him, I'll cut Sweeney's throat because I am very fond of the cock, and he makes a good pet. I hadn't time to go and get it before we sailed. Furthermore, I was going to let Cacalia keep him for awhile until we returned so she could fatten him up and give him more greens than he can get on the ship.

The same night one of the crew came back with a two-week old puppy. He is an engaging fellow, and I think everyone is going to like him.

I often wish I were in the European Theatre so I would get a chance to see some of the ancient centers of learning and culture. Shot up and bombed though many of them are, there surely are many things left of interest. All the boys in Italy get to Rome sooner or later; then there are London and Paris—and lots of other places.

But I wouldn't turn down the opportunity of seeing the East, and of trying to solve the mysteries of oriental behavior. What is so often mistaken for apathy is actually reserve and a lack of interest in commercial affairs and a willingness to live simply and without the labor involved in a highly mechanized state.

Philippinos in this port like to stay out of the sun, eat a little rice and fish, sing and laugh and do their laundry. The open market would scandalize the Findlay Market Association. There is no refrigeration, and the carabao meat hangs in red chunks covered with flies. The fish and seaweed and crabs and vegetables are handled in a most unsanitary manner. The city has open sewers and is alive with vermin. But in spite of all this, there is a charm to it, based primarily on the easy-going attitude of which these lapses are evidences.

I am enclosing a picture of carabao, which serve as beast of burden as well as edible meat.

From the very little news I get, I gather that the past few weeks have been momentous. Roosevelt, Hitler, Mussolini—dead. Surely this war is a victory for Russia, which rolls on in might despite its big losses.

Carabaos munch on grass

Carabaos in the village

"Don't look now but I think tonight's menu problem is solved."

17 May '45

How is everything with you? I suppose you can see the same quarter moon, and no doubt you had a sunset as glorious as we, although seeing it at sea with the Philippine hills in the background and other ships moving about in purple silhouette is a bit different.

We are in still another port this time, discharging thousands of barrels of aviation gas to keep the liberators and fortresses running. Last night when we were at the port at which we loaded, three of us went crabbing. We took flashlights and a car and waded through the swampy coastline flats where the crabs love to feed. In an hour we had fifteen crabs of a pretty good size, so today we boiled them. They are in the icebox, so for our midnight lunch we'll have the crabs and a salad made of cabbage, green onions, sea-grape leaves, garlic, oil, vinegar, pepper and salt. There is a Russian chief machinist's mate aboard who is a very companionable fellow. He loves to eat, and between us we think up some pretty fancy menus. Our galley is small, but it's informal, and anyone may go in and have what's on hand whenever he wants it. Oh yes, we will also have some tuba. We always keep some on hand. It is best when cold.

We now have an engaging little puppy aboard. She has just learned to walk and is just like a human baby. She cries if it gets rainy and she gets wet. Then you must take her in your arms, and she grunts with delight a few times, curls up, buries her face in some warm crook in your arm and goes to sleep.

Calbayog, my gamecock, which was returned by the thief Sweeney, passed out last night from the gasoline fumes, and we had to work on him to bring him around. The puppy took some interest in Calbayog and wobbled toward it confidently. The cock pecked her in the nose, and I don't think they'll have any trouble after this. Incidentally, Calbayog, I notice, is roosting high up on the yardarm tonight out of reach of the fumes.

My mail caught up with me last Monday—and I had about thirty letters. It was some fun.

Last week we were in Ormoc. What desolation! Sunken ships all over the harbor and all the buildings in the town in ruins.

On the way we stopped at a charming little village called Naval. No sooner had we anchored than the outriggers swarmed around. One

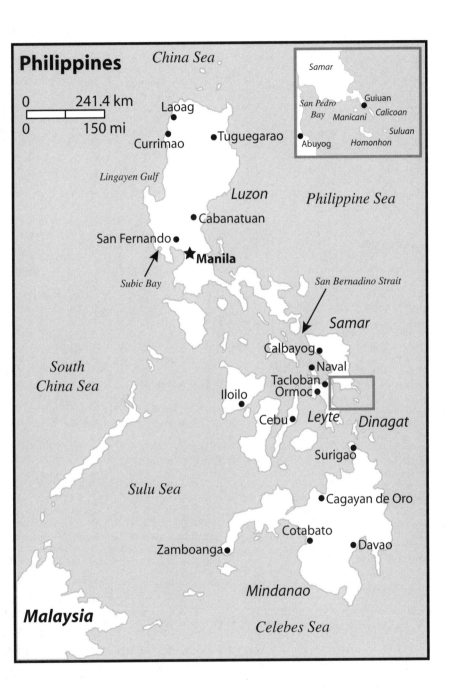

Philippines

China Sea

0   241.4 km
0   150 mi

Laoag

Currimao

Tuguegarao

Lingayen Gulf

Luzon

Philippine Sea

Cabanatuan

San Fernando

★ Manila

Subic Bay

San Bernadino Strait

Samar

South
China Sea

Calbayog

Naval

Tacloban
Ormoc

Iloilo

Cebu

Leyte

Dinagat

Surigao

Sulu Sea

Cagayan de Oro

Cotabato

Davao

Zamboanga

Mindanao

Malaysia

Celebes Sea

Samar

San Pedro
Bay

Manicani

Guiuan

Calicoan

Suluan

Abuyog

Homonhon

nice-looking Philippino hailed me and said, "Hello, remember me? I'm Frank." So I said, "Hello, Frank." He was aboard in a flash and said he was glad I came back because my wife wanted to see me. I began to get worried when he insisted that I was the one who had been to Naval last week and married his sister. To make matters worse, the whole crew and the officers agreed with him. Finally it was no joke, and it took everybody and the captain an hour to convince him I was not the person and that this was our first visit to Naval. It seems he confused me with a blond about my size on another tanker just like ours. Even then I was leery about going ashore, so a group of us went in case we were met by a party of bolo knife wielders.

We made a tour through the village. Pleasant grassy spaces surrounded by trees—grazing horses, goats, pigs, and the inevitable fighting cocks. Then we visited with natives (we were met at the dock by swarms of barefoot men and boys) who escorted us through the town asking us for "cigarette, chewing gum, hey Joe"—the cry of the Philippines. It was a relief to be in a town where there are no motor vehicles, no sailors, no soldiers, no jeeps and trucks, and no SPs pushing you around just when the fun begins. We ate pig and drank tuba and bought all the onions we could find and a stock of bananas. We knew we would be back on Saturday, so we ordered two roasting pigs, 12 quarts of tuba, 100 cigars (these had to be made), and left for the ship. We weighed anchor early in the morning and set out for Ormoc where there is a PT base. We unloaded all night, and many of us fished. I caught one small fish.

When we returned to Naval, we spent the afternoon swimming and lying in the sun. A native brought out a beautiful parrot, but they are hard to keep on a ship. They blow over the side so easily. About five thirty we went ashore. There were the boys, and the man from whom we bought the pigs. We went to his house, and began on the ever-present tuba. Soon three older men arrived in khaki undershirts and pants of a sort. One was the mayor, and he was rather well on the way to the Philippine equivalent of an Irishman's Saturday night. One of the other men has a son who has been a chief officer's steward in the U.S. Navy for 18 years and is now serving on a submarine (which pays 50 percent extra). He sends the old man $100 a month, which makes him the undisputed financier of Naval. The other man was quiet, glassy-eyed and with a fixed grin. He was definitely a constituent of the mayor, for he agreed with everything the mayor mumbled. After quite a feast—the pig was delicious, we also had the liver and the chitlins and mounds of rice—we were invited to the mayor's house for coffee. The coffee turned out to be whiskey, and it was very delicious. By this time the mayor was ready to give us the town, and when the Russian chief presented him with a flashlight, his eyes watered more than ever, and he clapped his hands three times whereupon three women of his house, which is partly a granary and partly a general warehouse and bedroom all in one, appeared with armfuls of whiskey. It was a Chinese brand and highly prized. It was quite an evening, and we were all glad we had a native pilot (they are hired by the U.S.) aboard to guide us through the narrow straits between Samar and Leyte.

Sunday was a lovely day and the scenery on either hand green and lush. The straits were full of native sailboats and the fishermen who squat in their canoes by the hour.

National gamecock fighting

18 May '45

Today we returned to what more or less seems to be our home base. The Philippine headquarters of the Coast Guard are located here. I'm happy aboard this ship. The size of a tanker's crew is never large because there is not so much work. An LST is a real workhorse. In peacetime a tanker could operate with eight or nine men. In wartime all ships must have more men in order to operate the guns.

We did some firing with our carbines at sharks and porpoises the other day. Lots of fun. Today I pickled some pig's feet—boiled the feet off the carcass we still have from Naval, and off the other larger sides we carry in the freezer. Then let them cool, poured off some of the water, and while still lukewarm put them in an earthen bowl with vinegar, onions, sage, bay leaves, and salt and pepper. They will be good with tuba.

Tonight half the crew went ashore to the naval base theatre for a USO version of *Oklahoma*. If the reports are good and we're still here tomorrow night, I think I'll see it.

The chaplain at the CG office gave me a very late copy of *Newsweek*. It tells all about Hitler's death. I must crawl in my sack and read it. Calbayog has gone to sleep, the moon is out, the water ripples softly by—and everything is properly set for an evening of rest and sleep.

27 June '45

How is everything with you today? Today has been another of those unmatchable ones—with sun and sand and surf and clean air and flying fish and nothing to do but enjoy it all. Lying in the sun all day, swimming whenever the spirit moved me, eating oranges and watching the clouds roll by. I took a long swim today and rolled around in the water watching airplanes, big PBY Catalinas, Hellcats, Helldivers—watched a big aircraft carrier push by and a proud cruiser cutting the waves.

Sunday the chief and I had a nice day. We called for Dinah and Maria Reston about four o'clock and walked to Santo Nino church, about a mile away, for vespers and benediction. They both looked so nice and clean and inasmuch as they are very pretty soon became the center of admiring attraction. You see, it really was something of a token of trust and belief on the part of the parents to allow us to go unaccompanied by older chaperones.

Going to church in a foreign land is almost bound to create pride in being a member of so universal an organization, and often I think, when I am in distant, strange places, that the only tie between myself and the atmosphere in which I sometimes find myself is the universal church and its material manifestations: the grass hut with its shrine, the thatched chapel with a bamboo cross, the crumbling pile of coral rock with its ancient pulpits, creaking burial carts, and tiny confessionals, the mission church of corrugated iron, and the chaplain's makeshift altar.

At Manus, the day I was transferred from the *169*, my birthday, I felt blue and lonely and sat there at a table in the club, overlooking the bay and the town around which the base is built. Above it all was the tremendous cross atop the new navy chapel. It dominates the scene—and yet the comfort that looking at it brought was not in the fact that the dominance was overpowering, but in the knowledge that when all this sprawling base has crumbled from age, that even if the national flag that flew nearby were to fall (God forbid) or be wrested from our grasp, that even when all the sailors and their small craft are things of memory to

the rocks and hills, that even when Halsey and Tojo and all the rest are in their immortal eras, that when the palms will sigh unheard in the breezes of the Admiralties once more, that no matter what happens, even the imaginative worst on Earth—that the Church and Christ will still be living, forever helpful. How can one feel lonely for long? It's embarrassing even to recall it.

I suppose June is deepening and the flowers of summer are going wild.

Maria Reston

11 August '45

Whatever you do with my stock transactions is all right with me. I suppose you sold just in time because I hear there has been a big drop in the market. Now with news of the atomic bomb and Russia's declaration of war on Japan, I suppose war stocks will drop still further.

We have been very busy—short runs, but are usually at the jetty at the right time. The setting is so idyllic that one could hardly ask for more than a place to sit and watch the mountains, surf, beach—and, oh, the sunsets. Take care of yourself.

16 August '45

I believe the Japanese have accepted the allied terms of surrender. The various half-true announcements that came out in the past several days have aroused a series of reactions and celebrations. I can hardly say that the news was at any time definite enough to allow for whole-hearted demonstrations, and by the time the word came that the surrender terms were accepted, the fervor had died down. Hence Armistice Day will perhaps be more memorable. The next and succeeding days were as subdued. Then just as the crew was showing signs of getting restless and talking about washing their seabags, the radio squawked something about ambassadors, and [James F.] Byrnes, and Switzerland, and about that time the soldiers encamped on the beach began firing bazookas and carbines and tent stakes, and this must be the real thing. So the captain ordered work and drills suspended; we gave several gallons of Pepsi Cola syrup to the army medics and accepted an invitation to a grade-A party, and almost everybody went ashore. Half the crew were temporarily AWOL, and the captain returned the following morning with his head under one arm and a kiki bird on his shoulder. Kiki birds are entertained as pets. They are supposed to whistle, but this one has either lost his steam or doesn't like ships because he just sits around humped up.

Armistice or no, we all know that there is lots of work to be done. The hundreds of supply dumps must be rearranged and simplified, millions of men must be moved, trucks and planes will continue to run for a long time, and there's the problem of doing something about by-passed strongholds. Just thirty miles from here 20,000 Japanese soldiers are pocketed. In Mindanao there are more. Throughout the Pacific and the East Indies the same is true.

Yet if this is peace, how significant that it should come on the feast of the Assumption, the Queen of Peace. Some decade this has been. What will the next one bring? And will the next war come in the third or fourth after this? History says it will come. St. Paul tells us that the only enduring peace is in our hearts.

Happiest of birthdays, Mother, from the Philippines.

18 August '45

Our mail has gone astray once more, so it will be a matter of waiting to hear the various news items and of the reaction to the Japanese capitulation. We get terse news on the radio and, therefore, manage to know what goes on in San Francisco at any rate.

The problems that face occupation, reorganization, reconstruction of Japan are tremendous. Japanese troops are spread over the Pacific. It will take years of hard work and difficult management to bring order and even complete cessation of hostilities in this area.

Meantime the duties to which we will undoubtedly be assigned can be tempered with the lure of travel, new places, new people—and in this case, a running study of the ever-puzzling-but-fascinating Orient. It occurred to me today that one of the essential differences between the East and West lies in the fragility of the East. Bamboo houses, flimsy dwellings, a life that permits easy moving, soft indulgent habits, the whole atmosphere of timelessness. Even the landscape, pearly islands, great mountains that seem to lack bases and weight. The music, the painting, the poetry are more of the spirit than of the solid earth. There is much to be said for a people who do not place too much concern in the affairs of mortal life.

26 August '45

Yesterday Stuart Hancock, the executive officer, and I meandered along the beach surrounded by the several pleasing characteristics, which make of this place such a paradise. The sun, the gently thumping surf, the salt foam spilling over the sand in restless designs, the welcome shade of palm trees, the mountains and pockets of clouds in their uppermost recesses and ravines, and beyond the beach and below the foothills in the fertile plain—the glistening rice paddies, squared and diked, patient carabao drawing ancient ploughs, and toiling Philippinos, knee deep in water and ooze, planting the shoots which are to supply the staple of diet for these folk.

Then we came by an army camp which has just been set up near the jetty to which we are tied. This outfit is a petroleum company fresh from

Europe, and we have made friends with them. These soldiers were in Africa and Europe for two years, and their transport, the Coast Guard-manned Gen. William "Billy" *Mitchell* (5,000 troops), steamed right by the U.S., through the Panama Canal, to the Lingayen Gulf. Many of them are disappointed at not having a leave, but like most army men they seem to take their reverses in a manly fashion. The average army enlisted man is, I believe, superior to the enlisted navy man in the manly virtues. Navy life spoils men by unintentional pampering in the form of prompt medical care, good food, good living conditions, clean surroundings, and a feeling of dependence upon the ship and its officers rather than on themselves. Certainly there can be no doubt in my mind that the man who must cook his own food, defend his own person, care for his equipment, carry it around, find his own foxhole, and who must learn to accept mud and mosquitoes with Spartan stoicism, is bound to be a more resourceful person than the sailor on modern ships. By comparison, the navy life is much easier, and I am inclined to think that this does not make men. Sailors are forever getting into brawls ashore because they are so pent up, emotionally, and insofar as conduct is concerned, they unconsciously turn to manufactured means of release.

1 September '45

It seems that my months in the Pacific are punctuated by so many interesting events and sociable times that the whole thing has been a tour—one that could not be purchased—packed with thrills, absorbing work, pleasant associations and stimulating recreation. I suppose it's no secret that a group of men from the same unit can turn on the heat, make the sky the limit and throw a whopping good time such as is possible in civilian life. I've been having my share. Nothing to worry about, no problem of driving home, nobody is left to wander about and get all fouled up, and if trouble arises you've always got a friend. Everybody helps the other, and there is an unwritten code to that effect. Even enemies within a unit are helpful shipmates ashore. Those men who complain about the service and keep talking about discharge all the time will find out, even in the midst of a recreated and devoted domestic life, that their years in the service were not wasted, or as so many say, "years lost out of my life." They may continue to refer to them as such, but the remembrances of countless hours spent talking over a cup of coffee will return again and again to the man who sits in the "freedom" of his office, who is "liberated" from the service and delivered into the hands of a daily routine, of commercial struggle, of dog eat dog, "I've got mine," "that's your problem," "call the doctor."

I hope I don't seem to be sentimentalizing about the service, but I'd just like to make the point that contrary to the idea that my time in the Coast Guard has constituted a yawning chasm in my life—the months I have spent in this uniform have been perhaps the fullest, and certainly among the happiest, of my entire life.

3 September '45

Yesterday the surrender was signed, and we heard part of the ceremony over the air. All pretty thrilling. I suppose everything is more or less settled, at least in the minds of the war-weary people at home. I suppose you are all glad it's over but uncertain about the future and its upsetting possibilities. However, if people can endure war, they can endure the troubles of making and keeping peace, although I must admit the latter is more odious to me because it is so vastly complicated and fraught with differences and difficulties.

As for us in the Philippines I suppose we will stay here for a while, as there are yet many uses for gasoline and will be for some time. I hope we get to Japan sometime before long. I think it would be very interesting to be stationed there for a while.

Everybody has been in a semi-holiday mood since the first reports of surrender. The Philippinos must think we're crazy, but they are so polite they'd never say it. Actually they are so relieved to be free of the Japanese—at least these people are—that they make all kinds of allowances and stay up so much later than they ever dreamt of doing. Anyhow, the night the captain and I went ashore, everybody got pickled to the gills, and I don't know how we ever got home, struggling across the narrow dikes of the rice paddies and through underbrush and all. The jetty is long and narrow, and the captain refused to try it. He had good sense and slept in the guard shack at the shore end of the jetty. Mr. Hancock and the army captain fell off the jetty onto a steel barge about twelve feet below.

They're both laid up now for four days. The sergeant, Chief White, and I, walking arm in arm, tripped over a coconut log and fell in a swamp, mud from head to foot. Oh well, it was fun, and I suppose the war *is* over.

We are underway, as I write, to Laoag, which is about ten miles from the northern tip of Liyou. The China Sea is really rolling, a typhoon having passed by here yesterday. It is moving north so we are in its wake rather than its way.

I don't know how I'll ever get my Japanese officer's sabre home. It's so long. Also my parrot (did I tell you about him?) who is sojourning in Tacloban. If the customs people see the parrot, they'll keep him in quarantine for 90 days at $1 a day to see if he has psittacosis, and then maybe I'd never get him anyway. I have a plan however: use a portable radio, take out the insides, put the parrot in. He will have plenty of air, no one can see in, and if he squawks, people will think it's the radio.

Enclosed is a special souvenir. Good-bye.

Lieutenant Fern, not his cousin in the German army

Rare bill

During Japanese occupation this would buy two pounds of rice

P.S. This bill is not meant to be a practical joke. These 100's are rather rare. During the Japanese occupation it would buy two pounds of rice or an empty Mason jar. The pictures show what happened to the Financial and Legislative buildings in Manila. The other picture is of a cousin of mine in the German army.

4 September '45

Tonight we are tied up to still another jetty at Laoag, on the West Coast of Luzon very near the northern tip. It is typical of the kind of mooring these small tankers are built for. Not much depth and lots of coral heads to dodge. The bay is very lovely, and since it is merely an indentation in the coast, rather than a protected harbor, the China Sea rolls in continuously, thrashing its blue folds into all shades of green, gray, and there's always the brilliant white foam. The beach is uncommonly broad and firm and makes excellent walking. The captain and I took a ten-mile walk this afternoon, and this walk offered so many lovely vistas and interesting rambles that I must recount some of them.

First of all we cut back into the jungle here and there when we could find a pathway, and many times we came into clearings bright with flowers, fragrant with catnip and alive with brilliantly colored birds. Later on we climbed over some sand dunes and came to the bank of a river that empties into the sea nearby. We followed the bank and came upon a bevy of happy women bathing. They shrieked with what was feigned embarrassment and engaged in lively chatter. In most of the Philippine places I've seen the men and women with their clothes on, and it looks so silly and uncomfortable. But in this area they haven't been badgered into a sense of shame, and it was refreshing to see uninhibited people for a change. Shortly they crawled out, put on their wrap-around skirts and pointed to their village not far away, suggesting bananas and basey (cane sugar wine). They were so friendly and most of them so pretty and shapely, we didn't have to think twice. We got to the village and went with three of them into one of the larger houses. The men folks were sleeping as usual and drowsily rose to welcome us and promptly reclined again. The little children were running about asking for chewing gum and repeating "Hi Joe," and "Victory," over and over. We then helped them pound rice

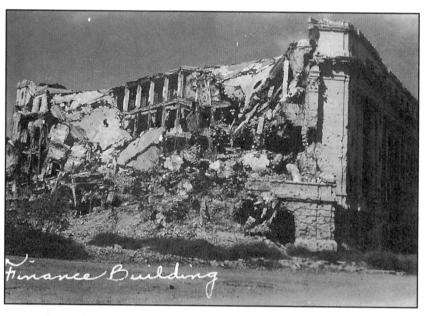

Finance Building

Legislative Bldg.

Government buildings in Manila suffer
the ravages of war, August '45

and shell corn, and shortly we were the objects of interest to the whole community. It was a pleasant hour in a village that has been untouched either by Japanese or Americans. This is a comparatively isolated area, and the only evidence of U.S. forces is the tank into which we pump our gas. From here it is piped many miles. Consequently, there are few soldiers to spoil the natives.

We made our way to the beach once more and followed it until we came to a wrecked Japanese ship. We went aboard, but the waves have pounded it so that nothing in the way of a souvenir was available. Then we came to an old Spanish tower, which is supposed to have a beacon upon it. We couldn't find the beacon light the night before, so we scaled the ancient ladders and found that the lamp inside the lens had not been replaced. Most of these lights were out during the war, but they have been restoring them ever since the Philippines have been "secured." So we'll report that fact to the Coast and Geodetic Survey, and they will print the fact that the light is missing in the weekly *Notice to Marines*, which lists changes and deficiencies in navigational aids the world over.

Then we came to the town of Currimao on the other side of the bay. Another Spanish fort and a large hacienda built by a Spanish tobacco importer. We went into the local church for a visit and some prayers, then set out on the return trip on the road that follows the coastline. Ox-carts, goat-herds, carabao (the indispensable beast of burden), little children, little horses, rice paddies, hibiscus, acacia, shaded road, native houses. It was a lovely trip, and we feel we've seen some of the hinterland of Luzon—all in all a real paradise.

We had a nice dinner: toasted cheese sandwich, real Italian salami, liverwurst, cucumbers, avocado, olives, grapefruit and tea. Then a mellow Philippine cigar and chatting with the traders on the dock—and now I'm ready for bed.

15 September '45

You ask about coming home. In the ordinary course of events I would have been eligible for rotation leave after 18 months, which would have been this coming November—eligible I say because actually the Coast

Guard has had a shortage of officers in the Philippines, and the chances even under the plan were not too good. Those people who did get home did a lot of talking, and lots of them did some stunts about their health, mental strain and all that. Now that the war is over, however, all that rotation is out for the CG Army Manning Detachment, and I don't have any idea when I'll get home, but circumstances being what they are, I don't see how it could be very soon. You can't just abandon all these ships and walk off, and, on the other hand, there is still a great need for fuel. Take Japan alone, with our great army of occupation, plus the Japanese, and Chinese—there will be a great need for supplies and fuel, and somebody will have to do it. And until some permanent arrangements are made, the people already in this area will have to continue their work. In this area of San Fernando alone there is a tremendous concentration of ships jumping off to Japan. They must be fueled.

Lingayen Gulf is as busy as if an invasion were taking place. I counted over fifty LSTs on the beach in this area—all loading men and materiel for the occupation. Brand-new tanks and guns, for we have more to do than merely occupy Japan. There is the threat of Civil War in China, and the presence of Russian troops on the border, and a thousand little simmerings that call for readiness.

I think that to the average civilians reading about the war, the din of battle was worse than to the ones actually in it because their imaginations held free sway and the thought is longer than the deed. So too, when peace was announced in the States, a more or less spontaneous feeling of relief swept over the populace, and celebrations sprang up with no trouble at all because to them war means fighting and danger and very little else. But to those in the area it is lots of other things: administration, medical care, life in a tent, on a ship, boredom, monotony, food, fun and laughter, dull periods, a life that approaches civilian existence in many ways— laundry, breakfast, mail, clean the icebox, clean sheets today, read the Bible, the magazines, ice-cream, a side trip on a day off, swimming, painting the gun mounts, target practice, filling out a fitness report, assign efficiency marks—every quarter just like in school, confession and Communion, a date with a nurse, a family dinner with the Philippinos, a few drinks before dinner—all these plus many more. It should be understandable why the announcement of peace does not come as a whirlwind. It is simply a fact, and it is apparent to us all that there is still lots to be done and that for those of us who are not too old and decrepit there are many months of the same life.

I must go on watch now—we're underway in the blue Lingayen Gulf.

27 September '45

We left Lingayen Gulf five days ago and arrived in Manila two days ago. We are anchored in the famous bay, and all I can think of is how much this part of Manila resembles the North Shore of Chicago.

Rumor has it that our ship will be decommissioned and turned over to the Philippinos. In any case the captain wants everything inventoried, so we have been rather busy the last few days.

Now that the war is over, everything seems to be in a state of flux. The men with "points" are going home, and most everything seems unstable. Mr. Hancock, the executive officer, and Mr. Strukbart, the engineering officer, are both married and going home for discharge. I guess the captain and I will be the only officers aboard for some time. When and if the ship is decommissioned, I don't know what will happen to us. Probably we will be put aboard another ship.

8 October '45

The executive officer, Mr. Hancock, has gone, so now all the paper work falls on me, and even though this is a small ship, there is more than you can guess. Only the captain and I remain aboard, and we have little idea how long that will be. Both the engineer and Hancock are on their way to the States for discharge. They have the necessary points. So does the captain, but he plans to stay in the service. I don't know what to do. If I can't get home, it doesn't make much difference. Moving the tremendous amount of troops out of the Pacific area seems to be a tremendous job and much slower than the papers would have you think.

You see, we have no yeoman aboard, and all the paper work, which I despise so, falls on us because we're the only ones who have a vague idea of what it's about. Transfer papers, health records, pay records, service records, quarterly marks, change of pay status, applications for allotments, stoppage of allotments, report of military personnel, voucher for increased allowances, national service life insurance, record of public property, report of absence on account of sickness, enlistment contract, application for leave of absence, pay record order, final medical certificate, designation of beneficiaries for death gratuity, report of medical relief, statement of creditable service, commissary report, inventory of stores— deck gear, provisions, engine parts, hull report, navigational supplies, ordnance, ammunition—certificates of dependency, notice of change of address, deck logs, fuel reports, cargo reports, war diary, signal logs, mast book, radio logs, secret and confidential publications. This and more— and there's some of it for everybody.

Then before decommissioning, everything must be accounted for— everything down to the last detail—the file must be corrected and arranged and turned in. All the endless personnel bulletins, detachment circulars, commandant's circulars, all unit letters, Alcoast, Alnav—memoranda, on and on and on. A yeoman who is trained in this can take it in his stride, but I never bothered much with it until the last few days, and I not only have my original duties, but all these plus the executive officer's other jobs, i.e., navigation and general management of the ship and handling of personnel. Fortunately for me, we have a good chief boatswain's mate, and he is the go-between for officers and men. He is a good leader and keeps the enlisted men on the go, prepares liberty lists and supervises the deck, the cleanliness of the ship, the laundry and all those details essential to one's living. I would be lost without him. He has had 18 years in the CG and knows what he's doing. The men don't like him, but good chiefs are seldom liked. A chief is the equivalent of a top sergeant in the army.

Manila, 600 yards away, is seething with the activity that is manifested wherever the military takes over. Endless processions of army vehicles, dust, confusion—and people, people, soldiers, soldiers. The harbor is crowded. Lots of Coast Guard ships, and as usual the club has been invaded by the always-ready-for-a-drink crowd. I've more or less had my fill of Manila and hope either to get to Japan or back to Lingayen Gulf, which is truly *himmel* [Ger. heaven].

Navy News
PHILIPPINES EDITION

Vol. 1 No. 30   U. S. NAVY DAILY NEWS   Thurs. 11 Oct. 1945

NEWS ROUNDUP

JEWISH WORKERS IN PALESTINE ON STRIKE

JERUSALEM (AP) - Jewish workers throughout Palestine left their jobs for five hours Monday in protest against British immigration curbs.

GERMANS EVACUATED; JEWS MOVE IN

FUERTF, GERMANY (AP) - German civilians have been evacuated from three blocks of apartments to make room for 1,050 homeless Jews.

GREEK CABINET QUITS IN FACE OF ELECTION

ATHENS (AP) - The cabinet of Admiral Voulgaris resigned Monday bringing to a head political strife brewing over impending national elections.

SAYS DEATH ORDER CARRIED DOSTLER'S NAME

ROME (AP) - A U.S. military commission trying Nazi Gen. Anton Dostler on a charge of having ordered execution of 15 American soldiers heard testimony of a German lieutenant Monday that the telegraphic execution order bore Dostler's name.

SAYS CEMETERY PURSE-SNATCHER CONFESSES

LOS ANGELES (AP) - Police investigator E.A. Russell says Abe Roseman, 46, confessed he followed funeral processions into cemeteries and robbed 14 grieving women by cutting away their arm-strap purses.

JESSEL'S EX-WIFE MAY WED CROONER

HOLLYWOOD (AP) - Comedian George Jessel's divorced wife, Elois Andrews, says she plans to marry radio crooner David Street.

KENNEY ON WAY TO AIR CONFERENCE

HONOLULU (AP) - Gen. George C. Kenney, Commander of the Far East Air Force, has arrived here enroute to Washington to confer with General Arnold on the future of America's air might.

WIFE MAY DIVORCE HERBERT MARSHALL

HOLLYWOOD (AP) - Lee Russell Marshall says she and film actor Herbert Marshall have separated and that she is considering a divorce. She and the actor were married in 1940.

Lack of Joint Strategy Worst Axis Blunder, Marshall Says

WASHINGTON, OCT. 10 - (AP) - Hitler, Hirohito and Mussolini made many stupid blunders but their worst was complete failure to frame a joint strategy, General George C. Marshall said.

This mistake cost them the war, he said, because the Allies did the opposite and pooled their resources.

Eager For Loot

"Here were three nations eager for loot and seeking greedily to advance their own self-interest by war, yet they were unable to agree on a strategic overall plan for accomplishing a common objective," the Army Chief of Staff said in his war report.

"The Axis," he added, "as a matter of fact existed on paper only."

May Have Been Decisive

Marshall said the dissension and non-cooperation among Axis members "may well have been decisive factors of this world struggle at its most crucial moments."

Here are ways, Marshall said, the foe helped the Allies:

1. Germany: Hitler's insistence on placing his own judgment ahead of the council of his skilled generals.

Italy's Puny Attacks

2. Italy: Mussolini's puny attacks on Greece and Egypt, forcing Germany to over-extend her armies.

3. Japan: Failure to follow up the Pearl Harbor attack with an invasion of Hawaii.

Excerpts from 11 October 1945, *Navy News,* on following pages

NAVY NEWS

TODAY'S SPORTS

Stage Set For Army vs Navy Baseball Fracas Saturday

MANILA--- One of the biggest battles in Rizal Stadium since the Americans chased the last Jap out of his hole, will come Saturday afternoon when the Third Brigade Seabees cross bats with an aggregation of minor league and semi-pro experts under the banner of the 513th. AAA Gun Btn.

Arrangers of the event expect that several thousand tan and blue-clad baseball fans will be on hand at 1400 to witness the first pitched ball of this Army-Navy affair. Naturally, there's no admission fee. The game was arranged as an exhibition natural when the Seabee team came through Manila, headed for games in Japan, Okinawa, and Guam.

Major League Players

The Pride-of-the-Navy Seabee squad, managed by Frank Oceak, a former Pittsburgh Pirate, has five players who report to big league camps this coming spring, and the rest are signed by top-notch minor league clubs.

To match this powerhouse gang, the Army came up with its 513th. All Stars--- who have polished off all opposition in this section of the Philippines. Their regular lineup, rumor has it, may be bolstered by men from other Army outfits.

So, the Saturday game will be one for sports-hungry servicemen of this region to attend and remember. All men, ashore and afloat, are invited to see the fun.

CHICAGO (AP)--- With Lefty Hal Newhouser slated to pitch for the Tigers, in the deciding game, the American League champions were installed by bookies as 2 to 3 favorites.

seen the Tigers stage another of their famous four-run rallies in the eighth inning to send it into extra innings.

However, all is lovely again ....and Big Hank is blameless.

ARMY'S 513TH.--Top: Tucci, Graff, Kelly, Dombrosky, Schloman, Choiniere, Bolster. Bottom: Beerman, Smith, Silvera, Reid, Finch, McGrath and Childt.

Gotham Roars Welcome To Admiral Nimitz

NEW YORK (UP) - Fleet Admiral Chester W. Nimitz arrived in New York yesterday and received a thunderous greeting—the first official reception given a Naval hero here.

Following quickly behind the Admiral were his wife and Rear Admiral Forrest P. Sherman, his chief of staff. Nimitz passed through a Naval honor guard and was greeted by Major La Guardia.

Five minutes after Nimitz's plane landed, a second plane arrived. It carried most of the 14 Navy and Marine Corps heroes who received Medals of Honor from President Truman

Tuesday.

The Admiral and his party walked to a 19-car motorcade which began the trip through New York. Millions roared a welcome such as a Naval hero hadn't received since the reception in 1899 for Admiral George Dewey of Manila Bay fame.

The Admiral's son, Comdr. Chester W. Nimitz, Jr., was found standing near the landing field. He had last seen his father a year ago at Pearl Harbor. He was invited to join the official party, but said he preferred to watch from the sidelines.

MOVIES TONIGHT

PHIL. SEA FRONTIER

Chapel--RHAPSODY IN BLUE, Joan Leslie, Alexis Smith
Captain's Mess--THOSE ENDEARING YOUNG CHARMS, Loraine Day Robert Young
Wardroom Mess--CHINA, A. Ladd

- - - - -

119th CB--STAGECOACH, John Wayne, Claire Trevor
35th CB--MY REPUTATION, Barbara Stanwyck, George Brent
Sangley Pt.--PATRICK THE GREAT Peggy Ryan
Cavite--THE PICTURE OF DORIAN GRAY, Donna Reed
APL-19--KEYS OF THE KINGDOM, Gregory Peck, Tom Mitchell
APL-8--XMAS IN CONNECTICUT, Barbara Stanwyck, D. Morgan
Wiseman--TOP HAT, Ginger Rogers, Fred Astaire
Panda--ROUGHLY SPEAKING, Ros. Russell, Jack Carson
Ship Salvage--SUSPECT, Ella Raines, Charles Laughton
Boat Pool--SALOME, WHERE SHE DANCED, Yvonne DeCarlo
Acorn 34--MURDER, MY SWEET, Dick Powell, Anne Shirley

Eisenhower May Succeed Marshall

LONDON, Oct. 8 -(UP)- General Dwight D. Eisenhower, 54, who led Allied armies to victories in Europe, will be named U. S. Army Chief of Staff within a few weeks, replacing Gen. George C. Marshall, a veteran of 43 years of Army service, a qualified informant said today.

Eisenhower, now serving as commander of American-occupied Germany will leave Europe about Oct. 31 for Washington, and almost immediately assume the duties of the 65-year-old Marshall, who has served as chief of staff since September, 1939, a high army source revealed. (In Washington, the War Department declined comment on the London reports.)

CHICAGO, (UP) Baseball commissioner A. B. (Happy) Chandler said yesterday he had resigned as U.S. senator from Kentucky.

118 SAILORS POOL CASH, HIRE 5 AIRLINERS, TO GET HOME QUICKLY

LONG BEACH, CALIF. (AP) A unique "aerial share the ride" plan was put into operation by 118 sailors homeward bound on leave from the USS Astoria.

The sailors, desiring to spend as much time at home as possible, pooled their money and chartered five airliners.

The flight terminates at New York City, with intermediate stopovers enroute to enable men to drop off at points nearest their homes.

LATE FLASHES

WASHINGTON, -(AP)- The navy has released 208,000 men since demobilization began six weeks ago, according to a navy department spokesman. In the first six days of October, he said, 60,000 were discharged..

PEARL HARBOR, OCT. 9 -(AP)--
The carrier Saratoga will sail tomorrow for San Francisco on her third trip to the United States since the war ended, with 3,800 veterans eligible for discharges.

SEATTLE, OCT. 9 -(AP)- Named for three brothers, navy sailors, who gave their lives in the war, the destroyer, Hollister was launched here today.

BALBOA, CANAL ZONE (AP) - All 48 units of the First Carrier Task Force, including seven battleships, seven airplane carriers, four cruisers and 30 destroyers headed by Vice Adm. Frederick Sherman's flagship, the Enterprise, are expected to complete the journey through the Panama Canal by tomorrow.

SAN DIEGO (UP) - Rear Admiral Edward U. Reed, (MC) USN, of Los Angeles, has arrived here to take over the duties as President of the Naval Retiring Board at the U.S. Naval Hospital.

SAIPAN SLAYINGS BRING STIFF ACTION BY SENATE

WASHINGTON, (AP) A double slaying by navy men at Saipan last spring has resulted in the Senate passing a bill to impose life imprisonment or death on any person in the navy who commits murder or rape outside the U.S.

11 October '45

Tomorrow is Columbus Day.

General Yamashita is being tried these days in the High Commissioner's residence, which is only a stone's throw from where we are anchored. Yamashita is the man who was in charge of the Japanese forces in Luzon.

I have met quite a few Ohio men—in fact, several who used to be in the 107th Cavalry, which was absorbed by several divisions at the outbreak of the war. Much of it went to the 1st Cavalry, which is, in the Philippines, dismounted and similar to infantry. Normally, if they did not still have horses, they would have reconnaissance cars, tanks, tank destroyers, motorcycles, etc.

I am rather anxious to get to Japan, but it looks as if we'll be sitting here for some time if the army, which owns this ship, doesn't get busy and repair the reversing gear. We can't function without it very well, yet they are so confused, and there seems to be so much overlapping of authority that very little gets done.

DAILY PACIFICAN

The Army Newspaper   *In the Western Pacific*

Vol. I No. 120   Thursday, 11 October, 1945

THE JAPANESE army will be completely demobilized by Oct. 15, Gen. MacArthur has announced, and the troops shown above in a Tokyo street wait sullenly for instructions concerning their next move. An officer at left directs the processing for these men who are typical of Japan's beaten army. — Navy photo.   *(International)*

Marshall Declares U.S. Destiny Is 'Prepare or Perish'

WASHINGTON, (AP)—Gen. George C. Marshall lifted the lid on an arsenal of "terrifying" new weapons and warned an America entering the atomic age that it must "prepare or perish."

To cope with the menace of scientific destruction and to "enforce our will for peace with strength," the Army chief of staff urged an intense scientific research and development plus a permanent peacetime citizen Army, trained and ready to take up arms —but "not a large standing Army subject to the behest of a group of schemers."

In a denial report to War Secretary Patterson, Marshall said the atomic bomb is not alone among the scientific advances "that make the possibilities of the future so terrifying."

Because "it is so important the people of the U.S. realize possibilities of the future," Marshall said. He asked Gen. H. H. Arnold, army Air Forces chief, to estimate the capabilities of modern weapons. Here are some of the hitherto highly secret developments Arnold reported:

"We can direct rockets to targets by electronic devices and new instruments which guide them accurately to sources of heat, light, and magnetism. Drawn by their own fuses such rockets will streak unerringly to the heart of big factories, attracted by the heat of the furnaces. They are so sensitive that in the space of a large room they aim themselves toward a man who enters, in reaction to the heat of his body."

Improvement of our jet fighters "may well produce within the next five years an aircraft capable of the speed of sound and of reaching targets 2,000 miles away at altitudes above 50,000 feet."

"Discovery of the secret of atomic power," said Marshall, "can be man's greatest benefit" or "it can destroy him." Then the General added:

"It is against the latter terrible possibility that this nation must prepare or perish.

"Atomic power will affect the peaceful life of every individual on earth. And it will at the same time affect every instrument and technique of destruction."

Daily Pacifican, Thursday, 19 October 1945

The bulk of the 37th "Buckeye" Division is composed of National Guards. The NG was mobilized in the autumn of 1940, and many of the 37th went to the Philippines, only to be captured in May 1942. What a long time for some of them. At the same time the 107th Ohio Cavalry went to Camp Forrest, Tennessee—then it became absorbed by tank units, the 22nd and the 1st Cavalry Division. Sometimes I wish I had stayed in the cavalry. I *know* I'd be a major by now. The Coast Guard is pretty poky about promotions, and now that the war is over, one might as well forget about it. Before the war was over, our captain made full lieutenant—he had been a jg for over 26 months. I've been a jg for 19 months.

Yesterday we went to the army and procured a motion picture projector. We got some films from the Fleet Motion Picture Exchange and had three shows, from 7:30 PM to 2:30 AM—part of it silent because the bulb burned out. But it was the most pleasant arrangement, and now I know I'll never enter a smelly movie house again. We had the screen on the fantail, under the awning, and chairs all about. On either side of the fantail, four feet above the deck, hangs a lifeboat. So I set up a cot in the lifeboat and used a life preserver for a pillow. Overhead the stars moved about slowly, the moon took a look, the lights of ships and shore strung a necklace on the horizon, and if I cared, I could turn my eye and see Bill Robinson, Lena Horne, Fats Waller, Ethel Waters, Katherine Dunham in *Stormy Weather*. Then Lionel Barrymore, Greer Garson and that wonderful Gregory Peck in *Valley of Decision*. Then all sorts of people in *Sensations of 1945*.

We don't have much to do at this point. I have lots of paper work, but I've just about cleaned that up now. Eat, sleep, go to the club, dance occasionally at one of the night spots, read, play gin rummy and wonder what's next. Happy Discovery of America!

15 October '45

Did you read the biographical sketch of Churchill in *Life* some months ago? What a complete man! The full life! Undoubtedly he is one of the prime figures in English history and probably the greatest man of our time. Only a big man could courageously change parties in time of stress—criticize his friends in name of national unity and health.

Next Saturday will mark my first anniversary in the Philippines. It doesn't seem so long. Guess I'll never forget the Leyte invasion. I had a letter yesterday from one of the survivors we picked up after the Battle of Leyte Gulf. He writes me every so often and is so appreciative of our efforts to make them all comfortable.

The sun is setting, and the lights of Manila are twinkling—the friendly Philippinos have paddled to the shore. Soon some coffee, a cigar—and the moon, the belt of Orion—and the lap lap of water.

PHILIPPINES EDITION	**Navy News**	SHARE THE NEWS When You Have Read This Issue, Pass It Along To A Friend

Vol. 1 No. 38   U. S. NAVY DAILY NEWS   Sun. 21 Oct. 1945

LATE FLASHES

NUERNBERG, (UP) - The trial of Nazisim's foremost surviving war criminals will open here Nov. 29. Notice of the date has been served on the bulk of the defendants in the Nuernberg prison.

LONDON, Oct. 19 (AP)----An unofficial world speed record of more than 600 miles an hour for a plane in level flight was claimed today for RAF Sqd. Leader Philip Stanbury.

BERLIN (UP) - The U.S. signed the war crimes indictment only after stipulating that she does not recognize Soviet Claims to the Baltic States and "certain other territories.

The stipulation was made by U.S. Supreme Court Justice Robert H. Jackson, Chief American Prosecuter.

WILMINGTON, DEL. (AP) - Admiral William F. Halsey arrived home with his family in nearby Greenville.

LOS ANGELES, (UP) - The Navy announces a "Demobilization Information Bureau" to answer questions of persons concerning service men's point status.

Homeward Bound

SAN FRANCISCO, Oct. 19(UP)-- Nineteen ships bringing home 22,840 Pacific veterans and released war prisoners will dock in the bay area today.

Three carriers, the Kalinin, Manila Bay, and Kitkun Bay will land 2,660 passengers at the Alemeda air station. Largest servicemen loads will be carried by the Monterey, 4,241, and the Sea Perch 2,310.

Missouri in Norfolk

NORFOLK, VA. (AP)- The U.S.S. Missouri has made Norfolk her first port call upon returning to the United States.

Wasp to Carry Troops

BOSTON (UP) - The carrier Wasp will be transformed into a troopship, Navy officials announced.

U.S. OFFERS TO HELP PHILIPPINES FISHING

WASHINGTON, (AP) - The national fisheries institute has volunteered to help pay the cost of training a number of Filipinos to rehabilitate the Philippine fishing industry.

Excerpts from 21 October 1945, *Navy News,* on following pages

Navy Eases Enlistment Rules

WASHINGTON, (SEA) - Men enlisting or reenlisting in the regular Navy now have the option of signing up for either two, three, four, or six years.

Instead of the four-year enlistment required since last May, the following options were introduced on 18 October;

(1) Seventeen-year-olds may enlist for either two or three years or not to exceed minority.

(2) Applicants aged 18 to thirty inclusive may enlist for two, three, four or six year periods.

Other Inducements

Other inducements are provided in the voluntary recruitment act of 1945 just signed by the President. These include:

Reenlistment gratuity of $50 in all pay grades for each year served in the current term of active duty.

Immediate payment of mustering-out pay.

Up to 60 days leave with transportation provided.

Extra Allowance

Permanent extension of wartime 20% extra allowance for sea and overseas duty.

Family allowances extended for full period of enlistments and reenlistments made prior to July 1, 1946.

Option is reopened for men in first three pay grades to receive either money allowance for quarters for dependants or family allowance.

Congress Cut In Spending Sets Record

WASHINGTON (AP) - The Senate Finance Committee voted Friday to cancel income taxes on wartime pay for all enlisted men, and agreed to give officers three years to meet taxes.

WASHINGTON, Oct. 20 (AP)---The House has approved without dissenting vote legislation chopping off government spending by 52 billion 653 million dollars. 5he reduction was made by cancelling appropriations and spending authorizations no longer needed because of the end of the war.

It was the sharpest reduction in spending ever approved by a branch of Congress.

The House rejected a rider desingned to speed demobilization. The added provision would have required the Army and Navy to discharge all men on application who had 18 months active duty since Sept. 16, 1940 (when the draft law went into effect), who had dependants, or who wanted to resume educations interrupted by the war.

LAYS STALLING TO ARMY IN SENDING MEN HOME

MANILA (AP) - Enlisted men, writing in the "letters column" of the Army Newspaper Daily Pacifican, accuse Army authorities of stalling, ineffieciency, and promise-breaking in sending veterans home. The writers complained that the Army was failing to make use of dozens of cargo vessels sailing empty for the U.S.

INTRAMUROS

THE INTRAMUROS has long been the heart of Manila. It occupies much the same site as the original city. Its walls have stood solidly since 1584 and even yet enclose the oldest university under the American flag, Santo Tomas.

Today the Intramuros bears cruel scars. Great holes gape in the ancient walls. Rubble mounts in grotesque piles. Fire-warped girders point skyward like angry fingers.

But life still beats. Native women sell bananas, boys smoke cigarettes, Americans grope inquisitively, cranes hoist supplies into neat piles--all within the walls.

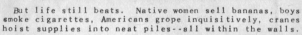

NEWS ROUNDUP

26 HURT AS TRAIN, LOCMOTIVE COLLIDE

GARDENA, CAL. (UP) - Twenty-six persons were injured and a motorman was pinned in the debris when a Pacific Electric work train, with 200 passengers, collided with a freight locomotive near here.

FORD TO BRING OUT '46 MODEL SOON

DETROIT (UP) - Ford Motor announces that its 1946 models will be presented publicly Oct. 26. Officials said price ranges may be 10 to 15 per cent higher than in 1942.

ADMITS SLAYING BRIDE "BECAUSE OF MOTHER"

DENVER (UP) - Joseph Desrosiers, 26, discharged veteran of San Antonio, Tex., has confessed he shot and killed his bride of 10 months as they drove through a Denver suburb "because her mother made life hell for us."

MARCUS NEARLY READY AS LINK TO ORIENT

GUAM (AP) - Marcus, a link in the proposed shortest all weather air route to the Orient, has been cleared of Japanese and will be ready to receive its first plane within a fortnight.

COWBOY KILLED AT MADISON SQUARE RODEO

NEW YORK (AP) - A 27-year old cowboy was fatally injured by a wild horse at the rodeo before an audience of 15,000 in Madison Square Garden.

UNCLAIMED BAGGAGE CENTER SET UP

All activities outside continental U.S. are directed by Al-Nav 328 to send all unclaimed baggage of Naval, Marine Corps and Coast Guard personnel to the Personal Effects Distribution Center, Farragut, Idaho.

BUTTER POINTS GOING DOWN, PRICES UP

WASHINGTON (AP) - Butter may cost fewer red points next month, but housewives are likely to pay five to six cents more a pound because of cancellation of a government subsidy to processors.

MOVIES TONIGHT
MANILA

PSF-DIVORCEE with Kay Francis and Bruce Cabot.

Wilson Bldg.- HOLIDAY INN with Bing Crosby and Fred Astaire

24th CB-THOSE ENDEARING YOUNG CHARMS with Robert Young and Laraine Day

119th CB-THE HIDDEN EYE with Edward Arnold, Frances Rafferty.

35th CB-MR. DEEDS GOES TO TOWN with Gary Cooper and Jean Arthur.

Sangley Pt.-BLONDE RANSOM with Donald Cook, Virginia Grey

Cavite-BLOOD ON THE SUN with James Cagney, Sylvia Sydney

APL-19-WHY GIRLS LEAVE HOME Lola Lane, Sheldon Leonard

APL 8-BREWSTER'S MILLIONS Dennis O'Keefe, Rochester and Helen Walker

Wiseman-ANIMAL KINGDOM with Ann Sheridan, Dennis Morgan

Panda-KEEP YOUR POWDER DRY with Lana Turner, Susan Peters and Laraine Day.

Ship Salvage-CAPTAIN EDDIE... Fred MacMurray and Lynn Bari

Boat Pool-THAT'S THE SPIRIT Jack Oakie, Peggy Ryan

Acorn 34-STAGECOACH with John Wayne and Claire Trevor

HEADQUARTERS FIVE MEASURES OPPONENTS

MANILA-- Riding on the crest of a winning streak, the CPSF casaba tossers Thursday evening ran the socks off Army's ATC Mustangs in the Service league, 66 to 8, then followed on Friday evening by defeating the strong LCT(GR81) basketballers, 79-33. Richart, Atkins, Feller, and Devick are playing mighty smooth ball of late.

The 19th CB's are leading the Top Service Manila basketball league with 8 wins and no losses. CPSF five is in second place with 7 wins and one loss.

(The NAVY NEWS Sports Editor would like to have reports from managers of teams at all Navy bases. Send them in after every game, and the News will print as many of them as possible.)

Japan Clings To Monopolies, Balks At M'Arthur Ban

Rebels Seize Venezuela

CARACAS (UP) - Rebellious army leaders overthrew the Venezuelan Government yesterday and seized President Isasias Medina.

The government toppled after a night of sporadic fighting during which the rebels seized control of the important military center of Maracay, 30 miles east of the captal.

Four of the five principal army garrisons in Caracas had surrendered to the rebels by mid-day, along with the Central police station.

Tank forces moved from Maracay to support the insurrection.

TOKYO (UP) - The Japanese Cabinet has balked at immediate action on Gen. MacArthur's demand that industrial monopolies be broken up.

The Cabinet discussed the demand for some time, but failed to reach a decision because "the issue has far-reaching effects on the people's livelihood."

Foreign Minister Yoshida said he doubted that dissolution of the old "Aibatsu"-- such family industrial trusts as Mitsui, Mitsubishi and Sumitowo--would benefit Japan. He said these monopolies built up Japan's trade up to a point where the nation prospered.

DISABLED VETERANS MEET

CHICAGO (AP) - The Disabled Veterans have opened their first peacetime convention in four years.

I'm enclosing a few pictures that are timely. A navy photographer gave them to me. He took them at the trial of General Yamashita. As for Brigadier General Grumer, remind me to tell you a story involving the two chiefs and myself and a quart of the general's champagne. I can't believe it when I think of it. Suffice it to say that we're lucky we're not all broken to apprentice seamen and in the brig. The building in which the trial is being held is within plain sight of our ship. We are anchored close to shore. It is the High Commissioner's residence. General Grumer is the judge advocate holding the trial.

The time I had in the cavalry counts on my longevity pay. I get five percent for every three years of service—so now I'm drawing ten percent of my base pay. Instead of $166.36 a month I get $175. For foreign duty (sea pay) I get another ten percent. (Enlisted men get twenty.) For subsistence allowance I get $21 a month. For a dependent mother I get $75 rent

Trial of Japanese General Tomoyuki Yamashita
High Commissioner's House, October 1945, Manila

Brigadier General Grumer

and $21 subsistence. Out of this I have $50 allotted to the bank, $50 to you, and $7.10 monthly payment on $10,000 life insurance (which is convertible). So what I actually draw in cash per month is $201.67.

Just three years ago yesterday I went to New London. Eighteen months ago today I left the U.S. Six months ago today I came aboard this ship. One year ago on the 20th I came to the Philippines. On that night all the ships in the harbor played their searchlights on the clouds.

30 October '45

Well, I'm more or less a transient again. The ship has been returned to the army and they have placed a civilian crew aboard. In accordance with decommissioning instructions, the officers (captain and myself) are to stay on board for a few days in order to acquaint the new people with a few mysteries.

I was promoted to full lieutenant the other day. Had a letter from headquarters. I feel pretty good about it, and it also means a substantial boost in pay. The rank is the same as captain in the army.

I sent my sword home. Also a seabag full of stuff—grass mats, etc. Continue to send mail to the *Y-44* until I let you know otherwise. It will be routed—I hope.

USS *Racine* (PF 100)
7 November '45—15 June '46

Patrol frigates were U.S. Navy ships manned by the United States Coast Guard. Originally authorized as patrol gunboats, they were converted to weather patrol vessels for distant duty. On 22 January 1945, PF 100 was commissioned USS *Racine* in Houston, Texas.

In September 1945, the *Racine* arrived in the Philippines to serve as a weather patrol ship. It was here in Tacloban where Lieutenant Fern, along with almost two hundred other crew members, was assigned duty aboard the 303-foot vessel. Their duty entailed 14-day patrols approximately 300 miles east of the south coast of the island of Samar, after which they would return to their homeport of Manicani Island for ten days for provisioning and any necessary repairs. While on patrol, *Racine*'s primary duty was to examine weather patterns and submit reports every three hours.

Lieutenant Fern compared life aboard the gasoline tanker with its minimal navigational devices to his new assignment on the USS *Racine* with its sophisticated anti-submarine warfare weaponry and complex communications systems. He relished this new opportunity to learn how to operate the specialized equipment available on his final assignment.

8 November '45

The *Y-44* has been turned back to the army. Philippinos are aboard, and I left Manila by plane, went to Tacloban, and was assigned to the USS *Racine* (PF 100), a frigate with 11 officers and 160 men. The duty is weather patrol—something new to me, and it doesn't look like Tokyo but should be interesting. We will go out on 14-day patrols and come into a homeport called Manicani, an island just off Samar. I reported aboard tonight, and we leave tomorrow. So the picture changes. You won't hear from me for at least two weeks.

P.S. Passed the physical for Lt. and the appointment was approved.

14 November '45

Here I am all settled again on the frigate *Racine*. I reported aboard last Friday, and now we're on patrol. This ship is designed for multiple purposes: combat, weather information, mid-ocean beacon, and air-sea rescue. We drift around a specific latitude-longitude position about 300 miles east of the south coast of Samar. Our "home port" is Manicani, a small island which before the war was nothing but a harmless little coconut island, but now is the seat of vast repair facilities. It lies across the bay from Guiuan and about ten miles from Calicoan. This is the principal navy center in the Philippines, and it appears that the bulk of its supplies and repair and maintenance facilities will be maintained here.

So far I like the ship very much. It is a class A ship, i.e., not of a supply or secondary nature. It is less than a year old—was commissioned in January of this year 1945 at Houston. Part of it was built in Cleveland, part in Chicago. It was floated down the Mississippi on pontoons (it draws too much to go unelevated) and was outfitted and commissioned in Texas.

The crew numbers about 175. Three chiefs. About fifteen first-class petty officers. We have a good laundry, barber, sick bay, ship's store, movies every night, and a comfortable wardroom. Best of all, the officers are congenial. I am fourth senior man aboard, which gives me certain rights that I am not above claiming.

At present I am standing watches with Than, who is my senior until I get on to the various devices which are new to me. This ship is a technician's dream and would strike a deep and sentimental chord in the heart of Charles Kettering, Thomas Alva Edison and possibly Galileo. It is quite a change from the tanker, on which we managed to survive with a magnetic compass and a barometer. Here we have (ASW) anti-submarine warfare devices: sounding machines, bathometers, depth charges of the "tear-drop" variety, the "hedgehog" pattern of anti-submarine rockets; about 15 different kinds of radio receivers, transmitters, inter-ship communication systems, loudspeaker PA systems, inter-departmental communications; hundreds of telephones; radar for air, surface radar, tracking devices, plotting devices, and biggest thing of all, Loran. All these, in addition to the ancient instruments, add up to something—and getting to know the bridge panels in the dark is like playing the organ blindfolded at the age of two. But it's all really very interesting, and I feel reassured because I'm tackling new things every day and getting along all right, so I know my mind isn't completely dead.

The ship is 303 feet in length, 37 feet beam, 2,400 tons displacement. The frigate is an old Revolutionary type (Old Ironsides), and I suppose this modern variety is but a sentimental nomenclature. The PFs in service number about 200. They are named for small cities, and when this one was commissioned, the mayor of Racine and his wife came down to Houston and gave the ship a motor-scooter (for running around supply depots) and $800 for books. (Either the books or the $800 has gone astray.) Anyhow the exec has pictures and clippings, and it must have been quite an affair. Mrs. Mayor of Racine ruined her new dress when the christening bottle broke the wrong way.

Our function is primarily to evaluate weather conditions and send in reports every three hours. This will go on at least as long as the typhoon season threatens with a demonstration. I've often wondered what we do after we warn all the other ships. A special group of meteorologists and aerologist's mates are aboard —and they spend all their time translating the mysteries of sea, wind, sky, pressure and temperature with reports for the consumption of ship handlers. This is a real CG function in peacetime. Weather patrols are maintained all year round. The Greenland ice patrol is well known: six months at sea below zero, then 30 days in Boston.

It's fun being on a ship that will move so handily. This one will make 21 knots, and it handles like a Buick. After an LST and a tanker I can surely appreciate the grace and movement of a ship like this.

It would be fun to get to Shanghai or Tokyo as a home port. But I doubt it. I had hoped to get over there, but here I am. I left Manila the day after I left the *Y-44*—by plane, and reported to the office at Tacloban. Stayed at the BOQ for a few days and had a good rest. Saw Maria—and my parrot, and had a nice visit. Took the parrot around town Sunday and back to the BOQ for a visit, then to Maria's again. Had dinner there—and left by LCI ferry for Guiuan (6 hrs) and caught the ship's boat to the ship.

Our patrols last 14 days. Then we are relieved by the *El Paso*—and stay in port ten days for provisioning and other necessaries. Sounds like it could get monotonous—but there is so much of interest aboard I don't think it will.

Well, I must get ready to go on watch and earn my pay—which now totals $372 monthly. Out of this I kick in $21 for food. Never felt so stable in my life.

Please take care of yourself.

22 November '45

It would indeed be nice to get home, but there is a point system in effect, and that's all there is to it. The 18-month rotation policy is no longer in effect, and there is no telling how long I'll be kept on duty in this area. You asked about weather patrol. The Coast Guard has always maintained weather patrols in the Atlantic, Pacific, and Caribbean. The prime function is to submit reports to a central station where daily predictions are made. Somebody said, "Do you go out and wait for a typhoon?" Well, it seems that way. Our sister ship, the *El Paso*, relieved us a week ago—

then promptly became involved in a typhoon. Her boilers were cut off by water in the fire room, so she had no steerageway—no power on the engines, or on the electric-hydraulic steering devices. Consequently, she was at the mercy of the elements and rode in the trough for four days. All her radio antennas were carried away, the emergency gear was soaked— so they could send no messages, and finally after searches by ships and many planes, she was presumed lost. So day before yesterday she came into port, while the base was instructing all ships to be on the lookout for wreckage. She was driven 210 miles off stations—the ships and planes never sighted her—the storm abated, they repaired their engines, and came in. They are tied up alongside us now, in need of extensive repairs. The wind went up to 140 mph, the barometer dropped to 26.90, the lowest I've ever heard of. The ship rolled 62 degrees one way, and they all had given up hope of surviving. But their experience reassures me about the fitness of these ships. If they can take that, they are all right.

Sunday we go on patrol again—for fourteen days, so don't expect to hear from me except at two-week intervals. I guess I'd better convey my Christmas greetings in this letter because I doubt if you'd get my next letter that can't be posted before Dec. 16 at the earliest because we'll be on patrol until then. We are also on air-sea rescue duty—with lots of special equipment, in addition to the weather patrolling.

Please take some of the money in my account and make some purchases if it's not too much trouble. I think Edward could do with a nice pair of gloves—calfskin or deerskin or pigskin. Virginia and Charles should have a Bible if they don't already have one. If not, I think a nice edition of Robert Louis Stevenson's stories is pleasant literary company. Maybe Louis can help you. Whatever you choose is fine. Louis should have a pair of gloves too. He has a big hand. Herbert and Quincy might enjoy several bottles of wine. Burgundy is nice, don't you think? Thank you, Mother. Give everyone my Yuletide best, and here's a big hug for you on Christmas.

23 December '45

Well, here it is almost Christmas again. A little while ago I heard the familiar carols over the air, and, of course, that always brings back memories of home and Christmas trees and the general air of expectancy and holidaying. Last year I was at sea en route to Hollandia, New Guinea. This year I'll be at sea too, en route to Manila, through the San Bernardino Straits. We'll leave Guiuan tomorrow afternoon. We are not going to Manila, but rather to Subic Bay, north of there. We must have a generator repaired there—six days' work—then go back to station "Sugar": 128 degrees E 14 degrees N. We had a lengthy patrol last time—were relieved five days after schedule. It was pretty rough most of the time, with an almost constant wind of 25 knots. About half the dishes in the wardroom pantry were broken, so we had to replace them at the large supply base here. The supply base is located at Calicoan, fifteen miles from Guiuan.

The rainy season has really set in. It seems that the Philippines have rainy season all the time, but from the winter solstice to the vernal equinox it really pours. Last week it rained for half of every day at least. Yet during the night watches when the rain beats in the face, and the voice of sailors howls through the rigging, all of a soft sudden the clouds break, and some familiar star blinks a friendly message as though to say: "Yes, we stars are still here; we've always been here; we're eternity; those storms down there on the surface have been coming and going for centuries. They blot us from view at times, but we are always here." Stars are so helpful and so companionable. One gets to know the procession of the stars across the heavens as they rise in the East. I always look for Orion to find out where I am and what time it is. Then if you find Orion, you can't help seeing Aldebaran and Bellatrix and Sirius and Canopus. Sirius is the brightest star in the heavens; it lies below Orion when it rises and is above Orion when it sets.

I think Sirius is what the Star of Bethlehem must have been. Perhaps it put on a special show that night. But then the ancient astronomers said that it was a new and strange star, and they knew Sirius as well as we do, so I suppose it was a complete phenomenon.

Happy Christmas.

Christmas '45

I hope you're all having a grand Christmas in all respects. Wish I could be with you all, but again I spend the holidays with my floating family. We're underway—through the historic San Bernardino Straits—route of Magellan and countless fleets and ships since, including the Japanese and American fleets in this war. We're clipping along at a smooth 17 knots—with a 30-knot wind to help, and by the 27th we should be anchored in Subic Bay.

I am in the wardroom tonight, writing this letter—and on this Christmas night we are abeam of the Tres Reyes Islands: Battassi, Melchior and Gaspar. By daylight we will be in the China Sea—bound north. We've had a big turkey dinner—the table was beautifully set—a little Christmas tree in the center, mince pie, ice cream, nuts, pumpkin pie, sweet potatoes with meringue topping, dressing, turkey, olives, cranberries, peas. At twelve o'clock I go on watch, and I'll be on until eight in the morning. Going through these narrow channels at night at this speed calls for one officer on the con and one in CIC (Combat Information Center); this last is a room with charts and radar scopes and range finders and depth finders. It's a big help and almost necessary at this speed.

The captain has just asked me to play gin rummy with him. I'm all for it because we always have a good game and lots of pleasantry. I know this sounds dull to many people, but life on a ship that rarely is in a position to grant shore leave imposes new meaning on otherwise small matters—and many words, expressions, and actions of a seemingly and ordinarily unimportant nature take on new meanings—and the business of getting along becomes a refined and refining process. From this point of view it would be hard to find a better group of officers. Everyone gives and takes, and all in all I think the eight of us present a nice cross-section of moods and temperaments.

Mabuhay.

10 January '46

Here we are in the New Year, and I hope all the best for you in it. The years are slipping by, one by one, passing into eternity. 1946. Ten years ago I started graduate work at U.C. Since then the world has seen many changes. Governments come and go, wars are begun and finished—and sometimes it seems too silly to be running around doing things when the whole business ends in a blur as far as this earth is concerned. I guess I'm the one in error. But sometimes I feel it's useless to do anything at all but just kind of sit around and wait until the next world. But then God surely made the world and us for a reason, probably to magnify Him, and as it were prove our worth, so I can't get by on that theory.

However, of this I am sure: if I didn't have the obligation of living up to some principles established toward the realizations of the immortal life, I would be the laziest person on earth. Of course if I had hunger to face, it would probably be different with me. But I really don't think, in spite of all my material advantages—my worldly riches—that I am married to the world we now live in, even though I partake of it heartily. I am one case of a person who has developed the other worldly point of view—because of riches, not in spite of them. I don't mean to say my actions are all moral in the Christian sense or that my actions are consistent with my convictions or that I am doing anything about personal sanctification. Perhaps I'd better do something about this preoccupation with the next world. I don't fear it enough. Maybe I should be more of a salvationist. I guess one's convictions are not enough. Still it's pleasant to dream and draw pictures of life after death. Maybe I should read Dante, especially *The Inferno.*

Why do people bustle about trying to do big things like building cities and highways and radio stations if they think they are going to live only the normal span of life? Maybe my thinking is becoming too Eastern. The Philippinos live in grass shacks and have big substantial stone churches. All the adversely critical say that the church is enriching itself and letting the people live in poverty. They want to see the *social* good. But they don't know what lies at the root of all this apparent lethargy and lack of concern about earthly surroundings.

All just a flight of my imagination. But most flights begin somewhere—like smoke.

We are now underway to Guiuan again, where we hope to pick up some mail—maybe Christmas mail, maybe some potatoes and other fresh things—then out to sea again on station "Sugar."

It's a lovely night—clear, a quarter moon, and lots of stars. We had steak for dinner, a funny movie, then hot chocolate—and at midnight I go on watch. I work hard on this ship, but the time passes quickly, so what's the difference?

We don't get any news—usually wait for *Time* or *Newsweek.*

24 January '46

Just after we left Guiuan two weeks ago for our patrol, the mail clerk delivered your Christmas package complete with holly sprigs and tastefully decorated gifts. It was quite a center of interest, this display, because few of us have received packages for this reason: fire in the P.O. at Guiuan destroyed over 3,000 bags of 2nd class mail (packages).

By the sound of your letters and those of others, so many men are coming home. Of course it would be grand to get home immediately, but when I think of all the boys who will never get home and all those who'll come home to live in a veterans hospital, I can't possibly find it in me to complain.

I have so much to be thankful for and now so much more in the way of associations, experiences, and new places—I can't quite fathom how I can be so singled out to have so much. Life has been good to me, and I often worry that I haven't discharged enough duty to compensate for the rights and privileges I have claimed. Maybe I'll try to even the score a little better in the years to come. Good night.

3 February '46

Thank you for the bars. They are so brilliant that I have managed to let everyone know that I am now a lieutenant without the least trouble.

The U.S. Navy and Coast Guard are strong on ceremony in peacetime. Even in wartime they usually have managed to dress up occasions of note, such as conferring of medals and citations, though I can only speak of that at second hand inasmuch as I have done only the ordinary work called for and not been in a position to distinguish myself, although I do know some people who have had letters sent in on their otherwise more or less expected performances and received special awards for their pains. For example, there is a Lt. Com. I know who got some presidential citation for saving the life of a man who fell over the side. Well, I guess that's all right, but seagoing people are supposed to save each other. I guess I might have asked the skipper of the *LST 169* to write in the time one of our boats fell from the davits. It was five o'clock in the morning when I heard the noise and happened to be up. The brakes had slipped in lowering this 10-ton LCVP, then caught, then the cables snapped, and the three men in the boat fell with it. Two of them were knocked unconscious, and the boat sank—and the people on duty were standing around like dumbfounded fools. So the chief signalman and I jumped over the side, clothes and all, and struggled with two men who were drowning. The third was still conscious and hung on to a line that was thrown him. We tied lines around those men, and they were hoisted aboard. No one bothered to thank us—it was routine. The fact that my wallet is still moldy from the wet does occasionally serve to remind me of the event. That was at Leyte.

Once in Hollandia, on a Sunday afternoon, we took the boat around to a little cove in order to find cat's-eyes. We couldn't take the boat all the way in, so we left one man aboard to man the boat, and four of us started to swim for the beach with our shoes on (because of coral). The beach was 200 yards away and the surf swifter than we had expected. The chief machinist's mate is a brawny fellow full of muscles and ashamed to be slow, so he started to swim with a vengeance. But his cigarette lungs caught up with him, and I towed him in some hundred odd yards. To get him back to the boat, I had to lash him to a log and push it against the surf until we reached the boat.

Then one time in San Pedro Bay on the way back from Tacloban, we decided to stop the boat for a swim. So the quartermaster got a cramp and called for me, and I am glad to know that I was able to save a man and spare a very nasty situation.

Then one night, also in Tacloban, when I was on the *Y-44*, the skipper (who can't swim) was very pickled and fell overboard. So I pulled him out.

Boy, is my back getting sore. Better stop patting it.

I was talking about ceremonies in the navy. Much of it is a buildup to obtain and preserve discipline. Smart appearance instills pride in a ship and the men on it, and, in turn, this nourishes willingness to perform in accordance with the ideals set. Discipline invokes an emulation of the officers, and much of the honor is directed to them. There are some interesting chapters in a book called *Naval Customs, Traditions and Usage*, by Lovette, which you should be able to find in the bookroom.

The news we get of all the strikes is very discouraging, and the letters we receive from returned members of the crew are anything but bright. They speak of strikes, housing difficulties, transportation problems, etc., and two of them from this ship who swore they would never forgive the service for its onslaught into their young lives have reenlisted in the Coast Guard.

There is nothing to do or see in this port. Of course, it's always nice to sit under the palm trees and have a drink. But that gets tiring too. If it weren't for the congenial officers on this ship, I would be inclined to junk it all and come home for discharge. But since I have been told in a letter from headquarters to stay on for a while, I guess I'll have to stay.

The other day we had a lot of fun at the club, which is, like many clubs, situated in a grove of coconut trees. I offered $50 to anyone who would climb any tree and get a coconut. I know my $50 was safe, but my, what a riot it was to see all these officers sweating and clutching in an effort to get even halfway up. The irony of it all is that any mess boy will scamper up and get a coconut for a pack of cigarettes. Shipboard life is not conducive to muscle building, and cigarette smoking ruins the lungs—so there you are. When I get the opportunity, I'm going in training. I feel so soft. I used to swim a lot, but the captain on this ship won't permit it. He is afraid of fungus.

My roommate left for the States, and he may pass through Cincinnati where his aunt lives. He is a nice boy, tall and skinny, and I enjoyed his company. It is hard to find just the ideal roommate, and I guess he was as close to that as one can find.

I hope Virginia received my Happy Anniversary cablegram, or rather my radio message that was turned into a message, presumably, at Washington. That is known as a class E message, sent over navy radio facilities.

I must go to bed—for a big day at the repair base tomorrow.

20 February '46

Station "Sugar," a point located at 14 degrees 00 North Latitude, 128 degrees 00 East Longitude, is my present location. Yes, we are on patrol again, having a rolling time and a pretty good one considering. We had a good steak dinner at noon today, and tonight we had spaghetti, meatballs, carrots, ice cream. Pretty good.

I had a pleasant watch from noon to four o'clock this afternoon. There's not much to do except keep within five miles of the position, so we drift and try to keep headed into the sea so everything won't be breaking up. I practiced blinker light with one of the quartermasters, took a few fixes with the wonderful Loran navigational gear, a few tours about the deck, and pretty soon it was four o'clock, whereupon I wrote up the log.

Robert Than, my "roomie," is headed for the States and discharge. Since he is gone, I took over his job, that of gunnery officer. There are so many things to know and learn in this service. The more I learn, the more I know I need to learn. Each field with which an officer is expected to be familiar, we barely touched at the Academy, but, of course, that is all they expected us to learn in four months. I have only the deepest respect for the regular Academy graduate. After four years they really know something. Fortunately for me, I have more time for study than heretofore on the other ships, and I feel that only now am I beginning to round out as a qualified officer of the Coast Guard. I have had more experience in deck gear, stores and commissary, recognition (strictly a wartime necessity) and ship handling. My experience in navigation qualifies me as a pilot, a little matter that I put to a test recently when I conned the ship in Bernardino Straits at night at 15 knots. But at celestial navigation I am still an amateur, so I mean to put some time in on that. That is when Loran comes in. You can determine your position out of sight of land with this amazing electronic development. Many of us believe that the developments in electronics—radar, Loran, sonar—are by far the most important developments of the war, whereas the atomic bomb is more or less a logical improvement in explosives.

So now I'll bury myself in big guns and trajectories and ballistics. The only experience I have had with weapons are the .30-cal. rifle, .45-cal. pistol, the 20-mm. anti-aircraft machine gun, and the 40-mm. anti-aircraft machine gun. On this ship we have three .50-cal. guns, depth charges, anti-aircraft guns, star shells, illuminating projectiles, and "hedgehog" pattern impulse charges used in fighting submarines. It's all very interesting, and I hope I can contribute what I like to call my intangibles to this practical field. Communications I have touched upon in a rather elementary way, so that is something to look forward to sometime in the future.

"In the future?" you say. I don't know much about it. We are supposed to be relieved of this duty before long and are supposed to report to

Pearl Harbor for new orders. What they will be we don't know. Naturally, we hope they will send us to the States for some reason, perhaps decommissioning, because I rate a leave when I can get it.

I wish I could get over to Tacloban to see Maria Reston and my parrot before long.

The wardroom is getting crowded, the movie is readying (on the fantail), and eight o'clock division reports are due, so I'll sign off and look at Sirius for you.

24 February '46

We had about two weeks in port last time in. There is little to do in Manicani or Guiuan except to consort with the other officers and go to the clubs, which becomes very dull indeed. Next time I hope to get over to Tacloban for visits with some of my Philippino acquaintances, not to mention Claudio, the parrot.

I am rather hopeful of getting to Honolulu before long. We are supposed to be relieved our present duty here by two other ships. But whether these ships are on the way, in the Pacific, in the Mediterranean, or still on the way in some shipyard, we don't know, for the message did not say anything about when.

I really haven't any news, but then I guess I never do. Just the same routine. But I think it worth mentioning that one could scarcely be involved in such a routine as this without considering with pleasure the truly palatable leaven. Certainly without the leaven of the good company of the officers and our ability to get along and have lots of fun out of very often nothing at all, this would be a boring assignment. Just for the picture I'll tell you a bit about them more or less at random.

At dinner, all the officers, except the one on watch, are expected to present themselves, with shining faces, and sit and break bread. We do, and dishes too, on occasion, when the party gets rough.

At the head sits Lt. Com. Clarence Waring, called "Fred" by his classmates, called "Captain" by us. He is a southern gentleman, academy graduate, aviator, well-read in law, knowing in engineering. He is 33 years of age. Lived in Antwerp for three years, attended school in England, college at Georgia Tech and Columbia. Married, one child. Lives in Scarsdale, N.Y.

At his right sits the executive officer: William Main, 35. Married, from Toledo, Ohio. Wife is a newspaper woman who knows Stewart Fern from Kent University. A real sailor. Very capable.

To his left sits Dr. Francis Boyer, PHS, neuro-surgeon. Married a girl from Greenfield, Ohio. One child. Loves to play bridge. Good disposition.

Now that my roommate has gone, I'm third-ranking deck officer, and gunnery officer, which is a good job involving lots of responsibility and administrative duties but not too much drudgery and a fair share of honor if your fire controlling is good. I have excellent petty officers in my ordnance division, and all is well and happy.

Then we have David Kierbow, Lt. jg, from Atlanta. 31 years old. Married, one child. Communications officer. Ten years service—an ex-chief yeoman. Loves to play any kind of cards and is my current gin-rummy partner. Then James Adams, Lt. jg., First Lieutenant. Young, enthusiastic, married, very capable ex-enlisted man. Been on the ship since it was commissioned. Lives in Oklahoma City.

Next is Ensign Carl Grummick, a healthy, broad-shouldered German boy from Baltimore. Very handy with knots and is making me a belt. Good hearted and wholesome. Unmarried, 24.

Then Ensign Eugene Gilmore from a small town in Michigan. A college graduate, very clever and a good sense of humor. Is an ex-reporter. Unmarried, 25 years.

The supply officer is Philip Lincoln, of the New England literary Lincolns. 31 years old, married; handles money but doesn't care for it. Always time out for a sandwich or a smoke and plenty of laughs. He and I don't like to go to bed early and get into long talks about everything.

The engineering officer is about 42. He is an old-timer in the service, is a permanent chief and temporary ensign. He is from Charleston, S.C., married, two sons. Very good-natured and constantly referred to as "the rebel." Knows his job. He is Charles Craven.

We have three southerners, three Catholics, one Mason, one agnostic (captain). The conversations are good and always friendly. The captain likes to discuss religion with me, and when he has a few drinks, always manages to rope a Catholic chaplain. I guess he is my favorite. He is such a gentleman, and even in his wildest times he remains true to a breeding that won't come off because it can't. Furthermore he is trusting and doesn't bother his officers unless he knows they need to be bothered—which, because of his attitude, is very seldom.

I guess it sounds silly to hear of practical joking, but under the circumstances of confinement and not too much hurry, it can be understood and forgiven. It's nothing to wake up and find a dead fish in bed with you or to be awakened by a cold pitcher of water. To gripe at anything is fatal.

Of such is my camp, floating, rolling, in the Pacific. After 12 months on an LST, six months on a tanker, I'm enjoying the comparative relaxation which this ship affords. I have more time to study, more time to read, and now with my extra stripe (it helps) a good job—it seems all a kind of fitting last chapter to this stretch of sea duty. I am going on the assumption that this will be my last ship before I get home for a leave. I should get a pretty good one when I get it, for I haven't had any leave since April 1944.

At present we are underway to assume patrol on a different station: station "R," or "Roger," at 10 degrees 30 N, 130 degrees 00 E. Station "Sugar" ("S") is being abolished, I suppose, because we were ordered today to leave it and proceed to Roger. One never knows the next move, but I have long since (in the days of the 107th Cavalry) developed the ability not to expect to know what may come or care too much. I consider wondering and wishing a waste of energy—my present store of which I am in need of replenishing, for it is 4 AM. Good night and good morning.

2 March '46

It is March already. We are underway to Manicani once more. Hope we have some news there about returning to Pearl Harbor. Wouldn't surprise me if the original orders had been cancelled.

I've just finished a good bout of gin rummy with our new supply officer, "Abe" Lincoln. He has a good sense of humor, and I guess he and I have more laughs than could ever be counted. He and I usually gang up on the two rebels and put them to rout.

Soon the growing season will be upon us or upon you. It is getting warmer here, as the end of winter approaches and the sun climbs north. On the 21st it will be on the equator. We are only 600 miles from the equator.

Church at Guiuan, Samar

"At Consecration, the sparrows burst into gales of song."

I'm writing this in the ship's office—which is pretty much messed up at this point. Today was payday, and although I don't see any money lying around, the office shows evidences of great past activity. There are a few stamps on the desk here. I'll show you a few samples.

These and many more. Lots of paperwork. It's staggering, but necessary. There are many files in here, two safes, three desks, bookshelves, copies of regulations, *Courts and Boards*, training manuals, pay records, health records, etc. etc.

What do you think of the service as a career? Give me your honest opinion. A new bill has been passed, permitting commissioned officers to retire after twenty years at one-half their base pay. It used to be thirty years or age 64. Twenty years seems a long time—and it would be on this type of duty alone. When I look back on past years, however, they have flown. It was fifteen years ago that I finished high school. That seems impossible. But there it is—1931.

One thing about the service is that it provides security along with the opportunity to live a life that carries with it a certain amount of adventure and respect. If one has a wife who demands that her spouse be home every night, I guess it's not so good, but then marriage to someone who demands too much wouldn't be very good anyway.

Well, it's something to think about in case I am given the opportunity to stay in. The Coast Guard isn't sandbagging anyone to stay in. The army and navy are begging for reenlistments, but the Coast Guard can't as yet. Its budget is too small. I must go to bed. Good night.

ps I'm writing this in the ship's office — which is pretty much messed up at this point. Today was payday, and although I don't see any money lying around, the office shows evidences of great past activity. I didn't get paid today. I thought I'd let mine ride for a while. I love to draw big amounts. Only I'll be careful not to go abroad in Honolulu with a roll of bills. There are a few stamps on the desk here. I'll show you a few samples:

USS ROCNE, (PF-100)   RESTRICTED

NO DEDUCTABLE TIME WHILE ATTACHED TO THIS UNIT

WARDROOM

CONFIDENTIAL

Executive Officer,
JW Watson

QUALIFIED TO WEAR ASIATIC-PACIFIC THEATER
OF WAR AREA CAMPAIGN MEDAL

SERVING OUTSIDE THE CONTINENTAL UNITED
STATES (OR IN ALASKA) THIS DATE

LESS THAN ONE MONTH

C. H. WARING
Lieut. Comdr., USCG
Commanding

c/o Fleet Post Office
San Francisco, Calif.

These and many more. Lots of broken work. It's staggering, but necessary. There are many files in here, two safes, three desks, bookshelves, copies of regulations, Courts & Boards, training manuals, pay records, health records, — etc. etc.

Samples of stamps

27 March '46

Spring is with us—and you—now that Aries is on high—and Venus sets in the West at twilight. Aldebaran in Taurus is red-eyed, and Mars in his sign of war and aggression is bloody and ready.

Just came in from a movie under the stars. Sometimes it's better to lean back and look at the stars than bother with what's on the screen before you, but tonight we had one I can recommend. *State Fair* is the kind of show that comes along as a godsend now and then, to clear the air of mysteries, war pictures, and the current vogue for gay-nineties look-backs.

Last week when we were in port at Guiuan, I took a two-day leave and went to Tacloban. I went primarily to visit some Philippino acquaintances and to check up on my parrot. All my friends seem happy and well, and I enjoyed being with them. The parrot is getting more familiar and now struts around and jabbers like the kind one sometimes sees in caricatures. Parrots are real comics. He seems to know me because he walks all over my arms and shoulders and nibbles my ears.

I enjoyed being in Tacloban again but found it very much changed. It was there that I had my first contact with Philippinos. The attitude of the populace is not the same. This is due in part to the lawless bands of robbers that roam around the hills, descending into the towns at night for plunder. The Americans are all rich to them. I was warned not to appear on the streets alone at night. A year ago one could go to sleep in the streets of Tacloban, and the natives would watch over you. There are other reasons. Last year the U.S. was doling out goods of all kinds to the natives; now the quartermaster dumps are closely guarded. Many of these robbers are alleged guerillas—armed, and some of them have been joined by deserters from our army and navy. There is also the matter of the American attitude—partly of contemptuous superiority, impoliteness, rudeness. Idencio, the steward on the *LST 169*, told me that a Philippino is very sensitive to unjustified rudeness and is most unforgiving in offenses involving a breach of good conduct, which, after all, costs only effort. Custom and tradition play a large part in their lives, and I guess our abrupt ways are often misunderstood.

It was a funny feeling, coming into San Pedro harbor and finding it so empty. Last time I was there was last November. I shall always remember it just before the final push against Japan—in June 1945. Over 1,600 ships in the harbor—of all types of combat and service craft. The other day—only two ships—and a great shining expanse of quiet water.

How is the honeysuckle on the bank? And the hedge? How are you doing in the stock market? I hope the tulip tree is progressing satisfactorily. Have a nice spring with plenty of dandelions and maybe a little bock.

6 April '46

Here it is my birthday again, and I guess I'm getting bigger. I expected a rather quiet and uneventful birthday but had a fine gift in the form of three letters from you. We have been out on station "Roger" for three weeks now because our relieving ship has had some breakdown, so the navy base at Guiuan sent out a tanker to refuel us here in the midst of the deep blue and the playing dolphins. Thoughtfully enough, along with 130,000 gallons of fuel oil, they brought our mail—so it was quite a day for us. We have run out of fresh food and have been living on canned things for some time. Even when we are in port, we do not seem to be able to get the good things we could when the war was at its peak.

The latest consensus seems to be that we will leave after this patrol for Pearl Harbor, then to Seattle. But all that is planning, and plans go awry. Ships have engine trouble, and the replacements aren't where they are supposed to be. I'll be lucky if I get home by midsummer at this rate, but I'm certainly not going to complain about a few extra months. I'm glad I came through the war alive.

The stars were so lovely tonight. First Venus set in a sunset glow, then the crescent quarter moon shone gently, like April. Then Jupiter rose in the East. I enjoy the evening watches so much. Usually I'd rather sit and look at the stars than go to the movies, especially if I've seen them before—and now they are reshowing all the old ones.

We fired some more VT fuzes the other day. They were one of the "secret weapons" until the end of the war. The results of the test firing are still confidential. The captain seemed pleased, and since this is the first ship on which I've been that has 3-inch guns, I felt rather good about controlling the firing and not getting all mixed up in a match of ranges and wind scale.

A year ago I left the *LST 169* at Manus. How time does fly.

14 April '46

I guess this will be my last letter from the Philippines. We are sup-posed to sail for Pearl Harbor tomorrow. Needless to say, everyone is rather excited about returning to the States. As I look out on this moon-soaked roadstead and the cliffs of Samar and the palms of Manicani and Homonhon Island slumbering and round and dark—guarding the mouth of Leyte Gulf, I say to myself: "What you, J.J. Fern, have seen and lived here lo these eighteen months!" Naturally it is with some mixture of re-morse and vague longing that I take my last look at an area I have come to know and like. I wouldn't choose this place as a prime desirable, but being here, one can make it mighty nice if he opens his eyes and espe-cially his mind.

Every time we put out to sea, we redesignate our beneficiaries and send in sailing lists to all concerned and in short, prepare for a watery grave. This time I went to confession to make the preparation complete. So if anything *does* happen, don't worry too much because my chances of committing any sins more serious than calling the captain a few ob-scene names are rather remote.

The April night calls, so I must go look at it and feel it for the last time in the Philippines.

Easter Sunday '46
At Sea—Guam to Pearl Harbor

Happy Easter! It is early in the morning—one o'clock—and the seas are breaking over the bow with real fervor, and the moon is giving halos to each drop, all for the resurrected Christ. I suppose the birds and the blossoms are outdoing each other in singing the triumph of our Lord.

I guess it won't be long now. We expect to reach Pearl Harbor by 30 April; I'll stay there a week or so for supplies and personnel replace-ments—then on to Seattle in May. I'm getting cold at the thought of it. I haven't been above latitude 22 degrees N for two years and after we leave Pearl Harbor, I guess I'll do some shaking. Seattle is 48 degrees N—above Cincinnati's latitude.

We stopped at Guam for fuel. Stayed there only four hours. It seems like a fertile island, as indeed are all the Marianas. I took my last look at the western Pacific islands as the sun dropped behind Guam. Wonder if I'll ever see them again.

When I first saw the Philippines, Leyte Gulf was quiet, mysterious, empty. During the 20 months of my on-and-off visits to that area I have seen over 1,600 ships anchored there at one time. Now when I leave (have left) San Pedro Bay—it is empty again, or practically so—and I feel as if I saw the Leyte episode from beginning to end. I encompass it all and treasure it as if it were all mine.

When we get to Pearl Harbor, we will probably find out what disposition is to be made of this ship: if it is to go on active duty again or be decommissioned or turned over to China. If it is to be decommissioned, I suppose I shall be finished with my work on here about the end of June or early July.

Tomorrow we'll have a big Easter dinner. Some of the boys are coloring eggs—with red lead, deck blue and assorted mixtures.

22 May '46

It surely was good to hear your voice again, Mother. It sounds just the same, inflections and all. It's nice to be back in the States, although I must say that in setting foot on this soil again, I did not experience the several surges of emotion that are said in some cases to consume the soul of the returnee. My first view of our soil was through radar. We could pick up land when we were 200 miles out. But even at five miles we couldn't see anything because of the fog. Our last two days at sea were featured by the foghorn and that strange quiet that prevails at such a time. If you have a chart handy, you can see how vessels approaching Seattle enter the Straits of Juan de Fuca at Cape Flattery. They pass the lightship *Swiftsure* and proceed through the straits past Neah Bay, Port Angeles. Then Port Townsend, and Indian Island, then past Useless Bay, Point No Point, Magnolia Bluff—and Seattle. Puget Sound is fine water, blue and clear and deep. The shores are green with pine and good grass. The glaciers did a fine job of carving out this harbor. No reefs or shoals to worry about and no buoys necessary. Seattle is a fine port. The city has over 125 miles of waterfront, which makes it a grand city for boating and bathing. The sound is full of large ships, naval vessels, merchant ships from all over, and hundreds of pleasure craft and sailboats.

The fog I spoke of predominates much of the year in the straits—but ends like a curtain at the entrance to Puget Sound. So there it was, all at once, instead of gradually—and I was home—nationally speaking.

One day last week we moved into a pier and loosened the gun mounts. Then a crane came along, and off with all the ordnance gear except small arms. Now we are at a different pier, No. 88, where we are busy boxing everything that moves or will move. Our ship is to be tied up someplace eventually in a practically bare status. It would be cheaper to sink it with everything aboard, but I guess public opinion is too much against that. We had dumped most of our ammunition at sea and set off the remainder at Indian Island (in the Sound) on the way in.

Today the last of the reserves were transferred off for discharge. The Coast Guard is not going to be so large after the war as it had expected, so 22 May was the date set for a deadline. Now we have 18 enlisted men, regulars, and eight officers, the latter of which only two are reserves—the exec, and myself. I don't know whether to be honored by this or displeased, but since so few are left and I had been asked to stay on by Captain Kerna in the Philippines, I guess it's some indication that I'm not entirely useless. Besides I like it. I guess I always will. And if I am eventually separated from the service, I'll feel as if I'm losing a way of life and a home. So get ready to readjust me if that comes about, and have a psychiatrist standing by. After four years of this outfit I feel somewhat like a college man about to graduate. Any effort that one makes to adapt oneself is certainly rewarded because I can truthfully say that I have enjoyed my time in the Coast Guard-Navy. It was navy for the most part, but the personnel was mostly Coast Guard. The operations were under navy direction. Two years living aboard ship with very few nights ashore. Comparatively small quarters, yes, but consider this: your work a few steps away. No transportation problem. No clothing problem. No food problem. Utilities for the switching of a button.

All that horrendous detail I told you about in connection with decommissioning the *Y-44* now must go on, but on a larger scale. And no yeoman, no storekeeper. There is lots to do, and the paperwork is staggering.

No steward's mates either, and the officers are going to take turns cleaning the wardroom, the head, the pantry. It will be lots of fun and not too much strain because we have a nice crowd of officers who get along well. We are moored close to the large aircraft carrier *Essex,* also the *Ticonderoga* and the *Hancock.* Close, too, are the battleships *West Virginia* and *Indiana.* They are being "preserved," preparatory to going in the 19th Fleet—the inactive reserve fleet. The guns get a plastic coating, and everything of a sealed nature is dehumidified.

On clear days one can see the majestic brow of Mt. Rainier's snow-covered magnificence. The Cascades and the Olympics are visible too.

I suppose the city is full of bloom and the celestial way. They say this is a fine time to be in Japan. I guess this letter sounds incoherent and mixed up. Perhaps I'm mixed up. Facing the termination of my service and uncertain about the next move. I am anxious to see you and Virginia and Edward. You've all been so grand to write so faithfully and keep me informed. I imagine that gets to be an awful chore for you, but your faithful and enlivening correspondence has been one of the prime sources of enjoyment. I guess you can never know just how much letters mean until you find yourself in circumstances in which there is little to look forward to except mail—and for the most part of the time spent in the Pacific, that was the case. Long stretches at sea and in isolated areas where there are no recreational facilities get pretty dull at times, and reading books and magazines and playing cards gets tiresome too. You can't imagine the excitement at mail call. I like to write to you—just talk through this same old fountain pen I had at the Summit. I bought a Parker 51 fountain pen at Pearl Harbor, but I don't like the way it writes, and it doesn't feel right for the thumb. Good night.

3 June '46
Bremerton

We are now in the Puget Sound Naval Shipyard tied alongside the battleship *Alabama.* We are packing all the loose gear and invoicing it to the shipyard.

I still don't know what my future is. I may be kept in the Bureau of Marine Inspection, I don't know. I guess I won't hear for awhile. At present there is talk about the Coast Guard manning the merchant ships if the expected strike goes through. Anyhow I'd surely be home for a leave in July—and a good one because I have accumulated quite a bit of leave in two years.

11 June '46

The decommissioning of the ship has now reached that slow stage comparable to the construction of a new house. The big things go hurriedly, making a very obvious change, so that one often begins to think that there is little remaining to do. But just as the little things loom so big later on in putting the finishing touches on a house, so do the hundred odd details of closing out an establishment like this become rather monumental. Much of it is somewhat boring and tedious, and the only reward in a job of this kind lies in the knowledge that everything is being accounted for and disposed of in a manner best suited to the wishes of the government.

The Northwest abounds in vacation opportunities and scenic delights. It is also a sportsman's dream. The hunting, fishing, yachting, rowing, swimming, tennis, football, baseball, horse-racing, skiing, mountain climbing, hiking—are all of the best and readily available. Some people complain of the large amount of rainfall, but I guess that's what keeps the grass so green and the flowers so bright. On clear days, the air seems to have a washed look. The snow-covered mountains on all sides lend distance and majesty to the setting. The clear waters of Puget Sound are like a nest of sapphires in the middle of green damask and ostrich plumes.

Every few days the decommissioning detail sets back the final date for hauling down the commissioning pennant. Now it is the 10th, now the 14th, now the 21st, now the 24th. Actually I doubt if it will be before the 30th, and then there is the "alert" which the unions have provided in the shipping industry. We may well find ourselves operating the ferries before we leave.

We're really seeing now what the peacetime navy is. Plenty of regulation and uniform observance. You don't have to beg for things and bargain like we did during the war—you either get what you want or you don't. In the forward areas in wartime many of the officers were constantly finagling to get something if they thought you had it. It was in many cases almost barter, and it shouldn't be that way. All the battleships and aircraft carriers are really something to see. But it is sad how depleted is the personnel. Most of them couldn't operate if they had to.

It's interesting to see how they preserve these large ships. Dehumidification is the keyword these days. Our ship is stripped of practically everything. In my department I have only a few spare parts for the guns.

Have you been watching the stock market? It scares me.

I've got several of the overseas small-print *New Yorkers* saved for the ride home.

USS *Racine* (PF 100)
The ship that "won the war"

21 June '46

Weekly progress report: As of 15 June 1946 I was transferred from the *Racine* to the 13th District, District Coast Guard Office, Seattle. Reason: Navy said all reserve officers must be off navy-owned ships by that date. Both Bill Main and I have left the ship—the last reserves to leave. It's all right because all my work was done, and the ship is scheduled for decommissioning on 26 June '46.

Meantime I'm hanging around Seattle, doing whatever they decide I should do. I still have some odds and ends to clean up in Bremerton, so I will be going back there a time or two. The personnel officer here is sending dispatches to find out what to do with me—and I imagine I'll be sent to inactive duty—with leave. I'll let you know as soon as I find out.

Afterword

Upon completion of his war assignment in the Pacific, Lieutenant Jules Fern was discharged from active duty, although he continued to serve in the Coast Guard as a reservist. He returned home to his native Ohio where he resumed his teaching career at the University of Cincinnati. He soon married and had five children.

Lieutenant Fern always spoke fondly of his days aboard ship, remembering them "as the best years of [his] life." He sought every opportunity possible to satisfy his persistent yearning to return to sea. On one occasion Bill Main, who had served with him aboard the cutter *Racine*, invited him to co-pilot the 53-foot yawl *Stormy Weather* in a race from Ft. Lauderdale to Cat Cay, and, although not prone to bragging, Mr. Fern never missed a chance to boast that they came in first.

With enormous pride of having served his country, Jules Fern retired as a commander in the Coast Guard Reserve in 1973. In 1983 he fulfilled another dream: to return to the Pacific. His visit was marked by time spent in Pearl Harbor, New Guinea, and Manila where he strolled with nostalgia among "row upon row of white crosses."

* * *

After my father's death in 1991, I discovered the box of letters and found them too colorful not to be shared with others. Thus—this book. I hope you have enjoyed them as much as I have.

"Row upon row of white crosses" photographed by
Mr. Fern during his visit to Manila in 1983